"I

Do

Not

Apologize

for

the

Length

of

This

Letter"

"I Do Not Apologize for the Length of This Letter"

The Mari Sandoz Letters on Native American Rights, 1940–1965

Introduced and edited by Kimberli A. Lee
Foreword by John R. Wunder

TEXAS
TECH
UNIVERSITY
PRESS

This book is typeset in Monotype Albertina. The paper used in this book meets the minimum requirements of ANSI/NISO Z39.48-1992 (R1997). ∞

Designed by Lindsay Starr

LIBRARY OF CONGRESS CATALOGING-IN-PUBLICATION DATA
Sandoz, Mari, 1896–1966.
    "I do not apologize for the length of this letter" : the Mari Sandoz letters on Native American rights, 1940–1965 / introduced and edited by Kimberli A. Lee ; foreword by John R. Wunder.
        p. cm. — (Plains histories)
    Summary: "The collected correspondence of Mari Sandoz focusing on her political activism in behalf of American Indians in the mid-twentieth century. Introduced and edited by Kimberli Lee, the letters document Sandoz's role as a non-Native chronicler and advocate for Plains Indian cultures"—Provided by publisher.
    Includes bibliographical references and index.
    ISBN 978-0-89672-666-6 (hardcover : alk. paper) 1. Indians of North America—Great Plains—History—20th century—Sources. 2. Indians of North America—Civil rights—History—20th century—Sources. 3. Social justice—United States—History—20th century—Sources. 4. Sandoz, Mari, 1896–1966—Correspondence. 5. Sandoz, Mari, 1896–1966—Political and social views. 6. Women political activists—United States—Correspondence. 7. Political activists—United States—Correspondence. 8. Authors, American—20th century—Correspondence. I. Lee, Kimberli A., 1959– II. Title.
    E78.G73S25 2009
    978.004'97—dc2   2009028080

PRINTED IN THE UNITED STATES OF AMERICA
09   10   11   12   13   14   15   16   17   /   9   8   7   6   5   4   3   2   1

TEXAS TECH UNIVERSITY PRESS
Box 41037, Lubbock, Texas 79409-1037 USA
800.832.4042 | ttup@ttu.edu | www.ttup.ttu.edu

For All My Relatives

CONTENTS

———

ILLUSTRATIONS

ACKNOWLEDGMENTS

There are several people I would like to thank for supporting me throughout the process of writing this book. They have provided encouragement, feedback, suggestions for revision; and most of all they've held good thoughts for me in seeing this to completion. First, I'd like to thank my parents, David and Dorothy Lee, and my daughter, Cheyenne Roy, for their patience, understanding, and love. Also, I want to thank Ina and Ate Charging Crow, and all my relatives in Wanblee, South Dakota, for their encouragement, as well as my Webster-Flores relatives in Macy and Lincoln, Nebraska, and my Black Bear relatives in Watonga, Oklahoma. Their faith in me regarding this project has been unflagging. I am also deeply indebted to Caroline Sandoz Pifer, Helen Winter Stauffer, John Wunder, Diane Quantic, Ron Hull, Don Green, Shannon Smith, Holly Boomer, and all my friends and colleagues at the Sandoz Heritage Society. This fine group of Sandoz scholars will always have my admiration and thanks for their encouragement and useful suggestions. Additional thanks are given to Judith Keeling and all the staff at Texas Tech University Press as well as the good folks at Purple Sage Publishing Services. Their help and good advice have improved this manuscript immensely.

Very special thanks are also extended to Malea Powell, Daniel Justice, Fran Kaye, Randall Popken, Christie Kellner, Angela and Eddie Ragan, George Wolf, Qwo Li Driskill, Susan Miller, Emily Wachsmann, Misty Thomas, Angela Haas, Melody Johnson, Rochelle Harris, Unci Anne Keller, Marilyn Tucker and family, Bill and Kathy Hagood, Tom Pilkington, Nancy DeJoy, Susan Applegate-Krause, Father Peter Powell, and Margot Liberty. These folks have supported me during all phases of the project. And although my dear mother Dorothy, Grandma Unci Keller, my Omaha sister Colleen Flores, and my mentor Randall Popken all have "walked on" from this world before this book could be published, they believed in the project from the start and influenced the writing of it. My mom read the manuscript in several of its permutations, and she always admired Sandoz's writing—especially *Love Song to the Plains*.

I am also indebted to all the archivists and crew at University of Nebraska Special Collections including Kay Walter, Mary Ellen Ducey, Carmella Orosco, and Kathy Johnson. I had help and support from the archivists at the Sandoz Heritage Center in Chadron, Nebraska as well, especially Sarah Polack and staff. Faye Nichols of the Gatesville Public Library in Gatesville, Texas, was always helpful and encouraging—she made inter-library loans effortless and dependable. I also want to acknowledge my appreciation for Laura Julier, Stephanie Chatham, Jill Kolongowski, Nicole Nyugen, Kristin Key, and Anne Taylor for editing assistance and technical assistance at Michigan State University. I am sure there are others I've neglected to name individually here, but I appreciate and feel fortunate for the help of all my friends and family in seeing me through this project. Anything done well in this book is because of your influence and support; all mistakes are my own responsibility.

———

Mari Sandoz was often asked to justify her writings and her opinions. That the question turned up most often when she was asked about her Indian books and articles was not lost upon her. On those occasions, she would frequently quote the Lakota, saying, "A People without a history is like the wind on the buffalo grass."[1] She would use this to make several points:

First, she did not think it was respectful or intelligent to deny the past. She herself had grown up in dire poverty in Nebraska's Sandhills and never lived a day without reflecting upon her experiences. Native Americans, she reasoned, had just as much right to a historical past as anyone else.

Second, Sandoz believed that her Lakota and Cheyenne neighbors had much to teach everyone about the Plains, the land, its environment, and their culture. To ignore or prevent the dissemination of this knowledge was in her estimation foolish and a celebration of ignorance.

And third, Sandoz respected all peoples and their history—when she wrote, she included everyone in the story. That her Great Plains was a grassland of tremendous diversity compelled her to embrace the stories of all its peoples.[2]

Sandoz sought critical acclaim for her work. She passionately desired success; and she wanted to be free to express her own political and cultural views. She refused to compromise her language and ideas, and her personal resistance to censorship carried over into her crusades against the suppression of ideas in America. Her own editor at Hastings House, one of her several publishers, noted her strong "concern for injustice."[3] She would not tolerate it. A preeminent storyteller, Ron Hull, longtime leader of Nebraska ETV and a close friend of Sandoz, described Mari as a "no nonsense woman." Sandoz was very active politically, and according to Hull she knew everyone in Washington, D.C., and New York City. And she knew most everyone in western Nebraska.[4]

This intensity for righting wrongs and desire to discover an honest past spread throughout Sandoz's histories and novels. Wanting every detail to be correct, Sandoz walked the terrain of history. She spent so much time soaking in the land that she became attached to the Plains. If she felt she was not making progress on her manuscripts, she was willing to start over. Rarely did she publish a book or essay that did not go through at least five versions. One of her books had fourteen full-scale revisions, and that was after she had destroyed a completed manuscript and started over from scratch.[5] She was also as tenacious an advocate as she was a researcher.

Mari Sandoz was born in the northwest corner of Nebraska in 1896 to Jules Ami Sandoz and Marie Sandoz. Both of her parents had emigrated from Switzerland to the Plains, Jules earlier than Marie. Before Marie arrived to marry Jules, he had married and divorced three other women. He was not an easy man to love as he was gruff and quick to express his anger with violence. Jules took out a homestead on the Nebraska frontier where he and Marie raised their five children, Mari being the oldest. Her father spoke French and German; her mother German. Mari herself spoke German until her parents were forced to send her and her brother Jules to a country school when she was ten years old. She then had to learn English.[6]

During Mari's early years, she grew up with the Lakotas each summer. The Sandoz homestead was near Pine Ridge Reservation; and although the blood of the Wounded Knee Massacre and the assassination of Lakota patriot Crazy Horse were still quite fresh, she and her father maintained a close friendship with Lakotas, who often visited the Sandoz ranch. While Mari's father went hunting with his Lakota neighbors, Mari played with Lakota children, becoming fluent in sign language and learning Lakota phrases. Although Lakotas were not allowed by the U.S. Government to leave their reservations, they came anyway; and the Sandoz family welcomed them. He Dog, Crazy Horse's brother, considered Mari Sandoz his adopted granddaughter throughout his long life, and she readily consulted with He Dog and other Lakota elders when she wrote her biography of Crazy Horse.[7]

Mari Sandoz penned numerous books and essays in her writing career. Plains indigenous histories include four books (*Crazy Horse: Strange Man of the Oglalas; Cheyenne Autumn; These Were the Sioux;* and *The Battle of the Little Big-*

horn)[8] and eight essays ("There Were Two Sitting Bulls," "The Search for the Bones of Crazy Horse," an introduction to *The Cheyenne Indians: Their History and Ways of Life* by George Bird Grinnell, an introduction to *A Pictographic History of the Oglala Sioux* by Amos Bad Heart Bull and Helen Blish, "The Far Looker [an Indian Tale]," "What the Sioux Taught Me," "Some Oddities of the American Indian," and "The Great Council").[9] Her fictional accounts of Plains Indians include two novels, *The Story Catcher* and *The Horsecatcher*.[10] Native Americans enter most all of Sandoz's twenty books. At the high point of her writing, she was considered by many to be the pre-eminent writer on American Indians. For that reason, when we think of Mari Sandoz, we often compare her to three other non-Native writers of the Plains: Annie Heloise Abel, Angie Debo, and Alice Marriott. Together these four writers helped begin the renaissance in Indian ethnohistory during the early twentieth century.[11]

But Sandoz was not content to merely chronicle the past. As a zealous advocate for Native peoples, she took on the federal government. She fought termination of Indian nations; and she fought the relocation of young Indians from reservations to far distant cities. She sought to make life better for those on reservations and battled fiercely with publishers to publish Indian authors and artists. She took to the new medium, television, to promote appropriate Indian causes; and attempted to forestall Hollywood's distortion of the indigenous past in its movies. Today the Lakota people continue to revere the works of Mari Sandoz. The late Vine Deloria, Jr., wrote an introduction for the latest edition of Sandoz's *Crazy Horse*. "Sandoz had an amazing ability," wrote Deloria, "to identify and develop themes and issues that plagued Indians during her time and that continue to disrupt us today. It was as if she had looked deep into the hearts of the people."[12]

To be an effective writer and advocate, Mari Sandoz developed an amazing system of record keeping, and she was a constant letter writer. She kept everything. Her interviews, her research notes, her extensive travels, her Native drawings and reproductions of maps, and her thousands of letters were preserved and deposited in the University of Nebraska Archives in Lincoln, Nebraska. Many scholars have benefited immensely from this rich collection. One other scholar, Sandoz's biographer Helen Winter Stauffer, published a general sampling of Sandoz's letters in 1992,[13] but as Stauffer herself says, they touch only the surface. Only a few of Sandoz's letters in that particular collection concern Indian peoples.

This collection of Sandoz letters focuses on historical accuracy and advocacy of Native Americans, edited by Kimberli Lee. Dr. Lee is the foremost active expert on the manuscripts and letters of Mari Sandoz today. Moreover, she organized the Sandoz Collection at the University of Nebraska Archives and presided over its microfilming, funded by the National Endowment for the Humanities.

———

Now it is time for you to read the letters of Mari Sandoz. If it has been a clear summer day and it is near sundown, take this book and a cool drink outside and soak in the wisdom of a writer with a cause.

John R. Wunder
Lincoln, Nebraska

"I
Do
Not
Apologize
for
the
Length
of
This
Letter"

Photo taken for 1950's *Flair Magazine* cover. Caroline Sandoz Pifer Collection, Mari Sandoz High Plains Heritage Center—Chadron State College. 2003.001.00057.

Introduction

I n 1943, shortly after her move to 23 Barrow Street in New York City, Nebraskan author Mari Sandoz was surprised by a group of young military servicemen who stopped by to pay her a visit. American Indian soldiers from the northern Plains region of her childhood, these young men were in New York to ship out to the battle lines raging in Europe. Sandoz invited the men into her modest apartment, and they explained that they had come to express their appreciation for her respectful writing about their people, and in particular her latest book, *Crazy Horse: Strange Man of the Oglalas.* The young men stayed for awhile visiting and later began to read small passages from her book about the famous Lakota warrior. Afterwards, they held a small honoring ceremony—speaking in their tribal languages and using the old hand signs as they passed the tobacco around. When they left, they each gave Mari the "double handshake of respect." She would later write her good friend Mamie Meredith that the experience was ". . . awesome toward the last. Somehow those young men, none probably over the age of twenty-four, had all the dignity and high seriousness of the old buffalo hunters left in them. It was the finest thing that could ever happen in my house, and I felt small and insignificant for a week."[1] This visit was momentous for Sandoz—it was then that she personally realized that the cultural traditions and practices of Native peoples were not vanishing and had not disappeared forever. In that moment, she understood that the "old time ways" had evolved and shifted in order to survive as viable practices for Indian people. The clarity of this event would significantly influence Sandoz's future approach to writing American Indian histories and stories. It changed her understanding of the adaptability and practicality of Native Americans—she had personally witnessed "survivance."[2]

It was equally important to her, I think, because she became aware that Native people were reading her work and appreciated her efforts. Having their respect meant much more to her than all the good literary critical reviews she could collect in a lifetime. This respect and appreciation has been remarkably consistent through the years, as evidenced by Vine Deloria, Jr.'s 2004 introduction to *Crazy Horse: Strange Man of the Oglalas*, and by the honor song sung for her at the 2001 dedication to the Sandoz Trail by the Sons of the Oglalas.[3]

Sandoz's writing career spanned several decades from the 1930s to the mid-1960s. She produced several works of fiction: *Slogum House* (1937), *Capital City* (1939), *The Tom-Walker* (1947), *Winter Thunder* (1954), *Miss Morissa* (1955), *The Horsecatcher* (1957), *Son of the Gamblin' Man: The Youth of an Artist* (1960), and *The Story Catcher* (1963). Though deemed works of fiction, these books are grounded in copious research and based upon real events and people. Two among them, *The Horsecatcher* and *The Storycatcher*, prominently feature Native American characters and storylines. Most readers and critics, however, agree that Sandoz's nonfiction books are her strongest works: *Old Jules* (1935), *Crazy Horse: Strange Man of the Oglalas* (1942), *Cheyenne Autumn* (1953), *The Buffalo Hunters: The Story of the Hide Men* (1954), *The Cattlemen: From the Rio Grande to the Far Marias* (1958), *Hostiles and Friendlies: Selected Short Writings of Mari Sandoz* (1959), *Love Song to the Plains* (1961), *These Were the Sioux* (1961), and *The Beaver Men: Spearheads of Empire* (1964). After her death in 1966, three more works were published: *The Christmas of the Phonograph Records*, *Old Jules Country*, and *The Battle of the Little Bighorn*.

Intermixed with this array of books, Sandoz also produced numerous articles, recollections, folktales for inclusion in various books and journals, and introductions to other works—most notably Helen Blish's *A Pictographic History of the Oglala Sioux* (1967), and George Bird Grinnell's *The Cheyenne Indians: Their History and Ways of Life* (1962).

Apart from Helen Winter Stauffer's biography, *Mari Sandoz: Story Catcher of the Plains* (1982), and *The Letters of Mari Sandoz* (1992); and Laura Villager's *Mari Sandoz: A Study in Post-colonial Discourse* (1994), very few scholarly books have been published about Sandoz. In 1996, *The Great Plains Quarterly* dedicated a full issue to Mari Sandoz and her work to celebrate her centennial year; but in the main, academic journal articles addressing her work appear only sporadically. In large part, the relevancy of her work and writing seems to be fading, though most Nebraskans still cherish her books.

Although her books clearly receive the lionshare of critical attention, Sandoz's correspondence and letters are of primary interest here. Given that her publishing career dominated the better portion of her life, it is a wonder that Sandoz had the time or inclination to produce any correspondence at all—but she did, much of it containing important historical information and research. My purpose here is to sharpen the focus on the letters Sandoz generated and collected during the latter half of her life, particularly those that illustrate and address her interest in and advocacy for historical accuracy in American Indian matters, political and social justice for Native peoples, and her active campaign to dismantle negative Native American stereotypes. Additionally, I want to direct attention to Sandoz's encouragement and advocacy of American Indian writers and artists. These foci illustrate that Sandoz was a respectful and responsible non-Indian scholar and writer of American Indian histories, and incorporated practices in her research on Native American topics that many writers and researchers could learn and benefit from today.

In order to achieve this purpose, it is necessary to examine these letters through literary, rhetorical, and historiographic lenses—a rather wide array of methodologies to be certain, but an approach Sandoz herself employed to a great degree in her own published works. Drawing upon the work and commentary of Native and non-Native scholars in these fields of study, I have attempted to create a framework to discuss Sandoz's correspondence that perhaps in some manner echoes her own. The combining of genres and methods to make a point or tell a story set Sandoz apart from the great mainstream of authors of her era and, in my view, situates her as one of the most vastly understudied, but unique and important, voices in American literature.

The Mari Sandoz Collection, housed in the Don L. Love Memorial Library on the University of Nebraska–Lincoln campus, is extensive and unique for a number of reasons. When Sandoz knew she was dying of breast cancer in 1966, she made sure to bequeath her materials to a repository in the West, with assurances that the materials would be kept together and available for future researchers. The University of Nebraska made those promises—now her files, vast stores of notes and interviews, documents, publications, manuscripts, maps, letters, personal library, and many of her awards, are safely ensconced there. It is a treasure trove of data and information, often found nowhere else, and still remains to a great degree underutilized. Recent construction of the Mari Sandoz High Plains Heritage Center on the Chadron State College campus in northwestern Nebraska and the gift of the remaining materials held by Mari's sister, Caroline Sandoz Pifer, have also added to the depth of archival materials that are now available for research and study. Both sites are rich in artifacts and information, readily accessible in important regions for any "Sandozian"[4] to visit in order to gain a sense of her life and work. Understanding her life or writing to any deep degree is well-nigh impossible without experiencing the land and environment of her childhood which shaped her writing style and her sense of *being* in the world. The landscapes of the northern Plains permeated the spirit of Mari Sandoz and her work.

Methodology and Editorial Concerns

My research into the Mari Sandoz collection at Love Library has spanned several years, largely concentrated during my doctoral work at the University of Nebraska from August 1998 until January 2001. As a doctoral student, I worked as a research assistant for the Special Collections and Archives to complete the Sandoz microfilm preservation project with support from a National Endowment for the Humanities grant. In the main, my job was to create an online finding aid for the microfilm reels, specifically working with Sandoz's voluminous correspondence files (well over 20,000 pages of letters), and her research card catalogue (numbering more than 32,000 cards). This finding aid for the Sandoz microfilm reels is available through the University of Nebraska–Lincoln libraries website. Duplicate copies of the microfilm reels of correspondence and file cards are available for perusal at the Sandoz High Plains Heritage Center in Chadron.

Already an admirer of Sandoz's work, particularly her nonfiction writings, I was eager to be immersed in the collection, recording and briefly annotating the card files and letters. My position allowed for learning several new important facts about her life; among the most interesting was the discovery of the many letters that attest to her personal advocacy and political activism on behalf of Native North Americans during the period from 1940 through 1965. Throughout those years, Sandoz wrote many hundreds of letters that relate to Native Americans, but I have focused on a selection of those letters that address her concerns with historical accuracy, her political involvement with, and criticism of, federal Indian policy, and her staunch stance against negative stereotypes and images of American Indian people (these were rampant in all phases of popular culture at the time including fiction, films, and advertising). Another important facet of Sandoz's advocacy for American Indians can be seen in the letters she wrote as an ally to young

I Do Not Apologize

Native artists and writers, encouraging them to develop their talents. Sandoz lobbied editors, art dealers, and others to recognize Native Americans' own work in these realms—much too often constrained, ignored, or unappreciated. The letters included here best represent Sandoz's thoughts and feelings on these four issues, and speak clearly of her commitment to Native people.

Knowing that her research materials, especially her correspondence, would eventually be of historical importance to future researchers, Sandoz carefully kept and preserved as much as possible, although storage of such a vast amount of materials became problematic. She had the foresight not only to keep the letters she received, but to keep carbon copies of the letters she wrote in response. This feature of the collection allows researchers to have access to both sides of the conversations and discourse taking place through the letters. Privacy and permissions policies restrict my use of the letters written to Sandoz, and so only her letters are reproduced here; however, the missives she received are available for study and research in Lincoln and Chadron, Nebraska. And though I have selected particular sets of letters here, readers will find that Sandoz's correspondence reaches into several fields of study and interest, especially history of the American West, Native American Studies, Women's Writing, Rhetorical Studies, Political Thought and Activism. Further, some of the letters contained herein may also be useful for those interested in the ethnographic study of Lakota or Northern Cheyenne societies.

As Stauffer did in her volume of Sandoz's letters published in 1992, *The Letters of Mari Sandoz*, I have tried to preserve Sandoz's own language and usage because those things relate to the reader something of the author's personality, intent, and the spirit of her work. We must bear in mind, however, that Sandoz was a product of her own historical moment; thus, some language and word choices may sound foreign or "politically incorrect" to us in the present day. In some instances, I edited the letters for content in order to draw focus on certain points within the letters, leaving out extraneous conversation or small talk. Larger excisions are indicated by ellipses in brackets; smaller portions of a letter's text (a word or a phrase) are noted with unbracketed ellipses. A few of the letters within the work here are perhaps a bit repetitious; however, I decided to include them to point out the subtle ways that Sandoz adjusted her writing and rhetoric to fit particular situations or address a particular audience. In regard to spelling variations of names, especially Native American names, a bit of explanation is necessary. At the beginning of the reservation period, agency officials sometimes altered family names (abbreviated, combined, or changed completely) in order to expedite the listings on agency rolls. For example, Sand Crane could become Sandcrane or Echo Hawk changed to Echohawk. I have kept to Sandoz's spellings as I found them in the letters rather than correcting or standardizing them here.

Arrangement of the material has been a struggle, but it seemed that the most logical framework follows a "chronological within thematic" organizational pattern. This means that the letters are grouped together by subject threads, and then within that grouping, they are presented chronologically by date. In this manner, the reader can get a sense of Sandoz's thinking on particular issues, and the evolution of that thought over time. This structure does not always suffice, however, as subjects sometimes tend to overlap. Sandoz often addressed both current and historic American Indian issues within a single missive, or discussed the political issues alongside the historical data.

Also included is as much of the addressee's information as was clearly present on the letter itself, although this data varies too because I worked from the microfilm reels rather than the fragile originals. Sandoz made a concerted effort to answer letters from fans as well as friends and she penned letters to many governmental figures, filmmakers, tribal members, and editors. Sometimes the recipient's full address appears and sometimes just a name or nickname. Basic data about the recipients of the letters are included in the endnotes to assist readers in gaining a sense of who the individuals were and their relationship with Sandoz, though in some instances these connections are vague. I have used no direct quotes from any correspondent to Sandoz. Endnotes are also included to help clarify the unfamiliar references Sandoz frequently used.

Beginnings: Mari Sandoz and Native Americans

Mari Suzette Sandoz was born May 11, 1896, in Sheridan County in far northwestern Nebraska, the eldest daughter of Jules Ami and Mary Fehr Sandoz. Raised in poverty on a hardscrabble homestead, she did not begin to attend school until age nine when local officials forced the cantankerous Jules to send his children to the rural country schools for an education. Learning to read had a vital impact on young Mari and she developed an abiding passion for it. She loved reading more than anything as a child because it gave her respite and escape from the bleak realities of her young life. Sandoz's childhood was difficult and oppressive, filled with endless work and the early responsibilities of caring for her younger siblings while her mother and father worked their fields and orchards.[5]

Her father, Jules, was a harsh and critical man, given to violence toward his wife and children. The abuse for Mari began early—her father once beat her severely for crying when she was just an infant; later, when she was twelve, she was severely punished for writing a story that was published in a Nebraskan newspaper on the children's page.[6] He was unpredictable and tempestuous, and never supported or encouraged his daughter's fervent desire to become a serious writer; he considered writers and artists to be the "maggots of society." It was only on his deathbed that he softened toward Mari and, surprisingly, asked her to write about his life. Glad to finally have her father's approval, Sandoz would go on to write the biography of her father, *Old Jules*. Ironically, the award-winning book grounded her career as a writer, but the specter of her father's maltreatment haunted her for years after his death.

Sandoz's relationship with her mother was not an overtly affectionate one either. Her mother seemed distant, yet intensely critical of young Mari. As the fourth wife of Jules Sandoz, mother Mary's lot in life was difficult, and the farm labor physically intense and exhausting, yet she managed to raise six children. Mari, as the eldest, became the primary caretaker of her siblings quite early as her mother returned to work soon after each birth. Sandoz chronicles the story of their lives graphically in *Old Jules*; upon a close reading, one gets the sense that Mari understood the hardships her mother endured. But the two never became close emotionally it seems, and Mary deliberately thwarted Mari's attempts to write of her father by throwing away most of the papers and letters that Jules had written and received as a young man. This situation may have served as a catalyst for Sandoz's diligent collection and preservation of her own correspondence; she knew how valuable such information could prove to be one day. Mary never recognized Mari's writing and research as "real" work, and like Jules, viewed such endeavors as impractical.

Sandoz remained, to some degree at least, emotionally traumatized by these family dynamics her whole life; she seemed to find solace in writing and research rather than in close interpersonal relationships, especially with men. Sandoz was briefly married to Sandhills rancher Wray Macumber; however, it seems clear this relationship was troubled and only sustained long enough for escape from her father's home. She never married again after the divorce, though she had other suitors. Neither did she return to the Sandhills homestead to live for any length of time.[7]

Clearly, Sandoz received little or no family support for or belief in her writing abilities as a youngster, but she did not give up her dream. Most of her childhood and adolescence consisted of harsh conditions, a hostile

Mari Sandoz as a small girl between friends Rose and Walter Flueckinger, taken in Hay Springs, NE. Caroline Sandoz Pifer Collection, Mari Sandoz High Plains Heritage Center—Chadron State College. 2003.001.00177.

family environment, and strenuous toil—an explanation why, whenever possible, she would retreat into the solitude of the Sandhills. Even as a child, she had great affection for the land and all of the hidden treasures nature revealed if one was patient and knew where to look. Out in the open spaces of the Sandhills, she could find peace and quiet, observe and explore the land, and allow undisturbed free rein for her imagination.

There were occasional bright times for young Mari, particularly when Lakotas and their Cheyenne relatives came to the Nebraska farms from the Pine Ridge Reservation only forty miles distant from the Sandoz homestead.

I Do Not Apologize

The Indians came for seasonal work on the farms, harvesting fruit and potatoes, and usually camped very near her home; it was well known as a friendly place to stay, at least for Indians. Not only did Sandoz relish the time spent with her young Indian playmates, she also enjoyed time spent with the adults and elders for they treated her with kindness and respect—affectionate behaviors she seldom experienced in her own home. In her introductory remarks to *These Were the Sioux*, Sandoz reveals that it was while she was still at an "unprejudiced age that [she] became aware of the Lakota's regard for children, [the] feeling that any little one, white or Indian, was to be considered as a grandchild, a feeling any . . . Sioux elder could rapidly convey to a child, simply by addressing him by the term of kinship."[8] And indeed, Sandoz developed close relationships with both Cheyenne and Lakota elders who addressed her as a relative. Among the many storytellers she would hear as a child, she relates that the Indians told some of the best and most exciting stories; even if she could not understand all the spoken language, the sign language the storytellers used aided her comprehension. These dramatic performances of story would remain vivid in her mind and no doubt influence her later writing.

The acceptance, benevolence, affection, and generosity she experienced among the Lakota children and elders surely held great significance for Sandoz and engendered a genuine trusting connection with them. The issue is complex, but I would argue that these early childhood ties with Lakotas and Cheyennes were directly related to Sandoz's perception that in many ways Native American culture was more humane and balanced than that of the Euro-American, and certainly worthy of respect and understanding. Further, I believe this feeling of kinship and consideration served as impetus for Sandoz's advocacy and activism on behalf of American Indian peoples that would take place later in her life. She felt she had a responsibility to the Native people of her region; and in fact to all American Indian people who had suffered at the hands of Euro-American colonizers. For Sandoz, writing about Native Americans was a privilege and an honor, not something she was "entitled" to do.

The Lincoln Years: Sandoz and the University of Nebraska

Although the experiences during her formative years were the germinating seeds for Sandoz's interest in American Indian culture and history, it was after she began attending the University of Nebraska at Lincoln in the 1920s that her interest began to expand and take on serious focus. Admitted to the university as an adult, Sandoz concurrently worked to support herself. She had various jobs while she attended classes, working in part-time positions for menial pay; she often lived hand-to-mouth—barely scraping by, but determined to stay in school. She spent most of her non-working hours writing, or in libraries, or researching in the Nebraska State Historical Society. She eventually became employed there as an assistant researcher to Dr. A. E. Sheldon, the society's longtime director, who was also interested in Plains Indian history. Here, Sandoz was given unlimited access to the society's holdings, among them the Eli Ricker Collection tablets and the Bettelyoun manuscripts, two vital collections of primary sources that would prove valuable to her future writings about American Indians. These collections, as well as the other primary materials she found in the Nebraska Historical Society, were crucial for understanding some of the early Indian/White relationships of the northern Plains in the late 1800s.

As early as 1930, while she was still a student at the university, Sandoz began revisiting her old Lakota and Northern Cheyenne friends and acquaintances with her friends Eleanor Hinman (who was also a student at UNL) and Helen Blish (an aspiring UNL anthropology student). Hinman and Blish were both working on projects focused on Lakota subjects and Sandoz decided to accompany them on the research excursion. Hinman and Sandoz set off from Lincoln, journeyed through Rosebud Reservation, and onto Pine Ridge Reservation to meet up with Blish; then the trio began interviewing and speaking with many of the tribal elders about Lakota history. Though Sandoz had been focusing on writing her father's biography and drafting works of fiction, this trip rekindled her interest in Native American history and culture. Unlike many white writers of her time, she judged the Indian point of view of the historical events to be valid and true. Conversation with the elders and other tribal members (especially He Dog, the close friend of Crazy Horse, and his relatives), crystallized Sandoz's determination to write sympathetically and respectfully about their histories. She believed the Native side of the story had been neglected for too long. Mari's sister, Caroline Sandoz Pifer, relates that in the process of writing each of her Indian books, Mari would often make a journey to the Indian country as a matter of course, to get a sense of the landscape and environmental elements as well as to gather information and stories from the Indians themselves. Caroline often accompanied her sister on the subsequent travels to gather data. It would seem that the first trip in 1930 established the pattern Sandoz would follow throughout her writing career.

This 1930 journey brought back memories of the stories that Sandoz had heard from the elders as a child and sparked her interest in the Northern Cheyennes' 1878 flight from the Darlington Agency in Oklahoma back to their homelands in the northern Plains. She took notes during the interviews with this goal in mind while Hinman gathered materials on Crazy Horse, the famous Lakota war leader. However, Sandoz quickly realized the Cheyenne project was complex, complicated, and required careful research. Trying to support herself in Lincoln in the worst of the Depression years, and with other projects percolating simultaneously, Sandoz chose to give priority to other books. After the publication of *Old Jules, Slogum House,* and *Capital City,* Sandoz was ready to return to the Cheyenne book in 1939. She was dismayed to find that novelist Howard Fast had been commissioned by Simon and Schuster to write the same story.

Sandoz's biographer, Stauffer writes:

Mari recognized the two books would indeed deal with the same episode. She considered the possibility of serializing her story to beat Fast into print, knowing she had the edge of using the Indian point of view in her narrative and all her notes were taken with that in mind. Ultimately, she decided instead to put her manuscript away until Fast's was "in the garbage dumps," at least ten years in the future.[9]

Frustrated and exasperated with this turn of events, Sandoz was surprised but grateful when her friend Hinman offered the Crazy Horse materials and story to her. Hinman, who had been working on the Crazy Horse research for some time, was not making the progress she had hoped, and felt Sandoz could get the work published in a timely manner. Though hesitant at first, Sandoz wrote to Hinman:

After thinking over the Simon and Schuster deal on the Cheyennes, and verifying the rumor that they hired a hack writer and chartered a plane to beat me into print, I find I can't go on with the book, which would only be, at the very best, a more considered work on exactly the same events.

Are you still disinclined to go on with the Crazy Horse story? If you are certain that you don't want to do the book, and that you will not regret giving it up, do you mind my switching from Dull Knife to your Sioux War Chief?

P. S. This time, no matter what I do, I'll not do the ethical thing of staking my claim publicly—not and have it jumped again.[10]

Sandoz dove into the work full force, determined to make this work as historically accurate as possible. She relocated to Denver to be near the best possible resources and repositories in the West, and travelled to Washington, D.C., to work in the War Department records and Indian Bureau files. She had to live frugally during this period, making ends meet with the monies she saved from her first three publications, and financing her research out of her own pocket. As she had in 1930, she then returned to Pine Ridge and the Black Hills for additional information and atmosphere—she wanted all aspects of this work to be accurate and the landscape of that region always inspired her creativity. Published in 1942, *Crazy Horse: Strange Man of the Oglalas* was dedicated to her good friend, Eleanor Hinman.

A Shifting Focus

Sandoz did not seriously resume her research and writing about the Northern Cheyenne's escape from Darlington Agency in Oklahoma until 1949. During this time she had the opportunity to spend approximately six uninterrupted weeks at the Northern Cheyenne Reservation in Montana conducting interviews and talking to the Cheyenne elders. Despite the fact that she was there to do historical research, the disturbing conditions of the people's present-day situation caused Sandoz to shift her attention to the ongoing hardships the Northern Cheyennes were living amidst: hunger, poverty, disease, and despair. This appalling situation served as a catalyst for Sandoz's political activism on behalf of the tribes. As soon as she returned to New York City, where she had moved after the publication of *Crazy Horse*, Sandoz penned a long letter to President Harry Truman detailing the atrocious conditions facing the Northern Cheyennes. This letter, and the rhetorical strategies it employs, would be revised several times in the future as Sandoz began her correspondence campaign against the federal Indian policies that were detrimental for Native Americans. It is this letter that inspired the title of the book you are now reading. I find it interesting that Sandoz had no hesitation about firing off a letter to the President—she, like her father before her, expected her views to be heard.

The rhetorical strategies she utilizes in her letters are varied and effective. She knows her audience and how to make a compelling appeal. In her letter to Truman, she starts off politely enough, but quickly calls on his sense of civic duty and sense of fairness for the tribes, who are after all a part of his

I Do Not Apologize

constituency. Sandoz also makes reference to an old Cheyenne holy man dying in his bed rather than traveling to the hospital of his "hereditary enemies, the Crows," and later calls up the image of the Cross of Christ—clearly a reminder that not only are the Cheyennes religious in their own ways, but also that the president has a Christian duty he should uphold in helping the tribe.[11] Likewise, she expected some acknowledgment (if not satisfaction) about this important issue. Truman, however, did not respond personally to Sandoz's letter. This did not deter her in the least—she was adamant about social and political justice for Native peoples and she would continue her campaign on behalf of the tribes. Various revisions of this particular letter would be sent to some of the most virulent promoters of termination policy—senators and representatives alike. These letters often conclude with a note or some reference to herself as a respectable author, the tone indicating she will not be easily brushed off or ignored.

Even though many situations surrounding social justice for Native Americans were frustrating and discouraging, Sandoz's personal involvement was unwavering as we will see in Chapter Two. Native American rights during the 1940s, '50s, and '60s were in their infancy. The National Congress of American Indians and the National Indian Youth Council would not reach prominence until the mid-to-late 1950s. But Sandoz kept a close eye on Native American issues during the 1940s, and by 1950, as the letters will show, she was deeply involved in advocacy for the tribes. She knew firsthand that Native people were being taken advantage of—many times with the sanction of those entrusted to look out for their economic growth and well-being. In a 1951 letter to one of her literary agents, she writes of an unnamed article she was working on:

> I am started on an Indian article, but it's developing a sort of personal tinge that you may not like. For one thing, all the publicity for the Cheyennes last spring finally produced some action in the form of fairly substantial payments on exploratory oil leases. This means, at the very least, a passably good road into the reservation and some temporary lease money, and there's pretty valid evidence of oil there, enough to toll in shady promoters who have been trying for four years to steal the oil rights by starving the Indians into desperation, with the connivance, I am convinced, of the oil representatives in congress. This was an aspect of the Cheyennes' problem I couldn't mention in my appeal last spring. But something started real action and now reputable oil prospectors have applied for leases the Indian Bureau might approve.[12]

Her activism and advocacy for Native people began to change her perspectives about them and her depictions of them in her works. Earlier in her career, Sandoz sometimes thought that the Native interviewees were being contentious and making research much more difficult than need be.[13] But slowly as trust was built over time, Sandoz came to understand that there were specific and serious reasons that the Lakotas and Cheyennes were reluctant to share their knowledge of past events. She was made aware of specific situations and given information from the Indian informants that she kept to herself and never shared.[14] As understanding and confidence strengthened between tribal members and Sandoz, her respect for Native American cultural practices increased as well. She realized the problems in Indian country were complex and multilayered, and could not be easily solved.

Her writing of Native histories evolved as well—what she once termed "oddities" of American Indians became traits she admired and advocated for in later years. In her earlier books, many times American Indians are depicted as "vanishing;" but in the late 1940s and on through the rest of her writing career, they are depicted as survivors. For example, at the end of 1953's *Cheyenne Autumn*, although they are only a "remnant," the Northern Cheyennes are still living and moving on toward their homelands:

> A trilling went up from among them somewhere, a young voice, a young girl come into a new time. Her thin, clear peal was followed by a loud resounding cry, a cry of the grown, the old, the weary, and the forlorn. But on the spring wind it was a cry of joy, of tears and sorrows too, for all those lost along the way, but a cry of joy. It had taken a long, long time, but they were home at last.[15]

This ending is one of hope, and a clear indication that the Northern Cheyennes will rebuild their nation. Fittingly, it is the voice of a young woman who is the first to cry out—as she stands for the "mother of the People," and ensures the continuation of Cheyenne ways. This ending is a significantly different one than that found in *Crazy Horse*, written ten years earlier. The book ends in cries, but cries brought on by sorrow and death. After being assaulted and stabbed by a guard at the Fort Robinson prison barracks, Crazy Horse lies dying with his father, Worm, and his cousin, Touch the Clouds, standing watch—the only witnesses to his last words:

> For awhile it seemed he would say more, then slowly his head seemed to settle back, the eyes opened wide, and one long brown braid slid to the

I Do Not Apologize

floor. Gently, Touch the Clouds replaced it, holding it on the breast of his friend with his strong hand. And in the yellow light of the lamp the two men wept, the tears like rain washing over live rocks, rocks in that old north country of the Powder and the Yellowstone, for the Strange Man of the Oglalas was dead.[16]

Clearly, both scenes were written for maximum dramatic effect, but *Cheyenne Autumn* ends with joyful sounds, hopeful survivors and a new beginning whereas *Crazy Horse* ends abruptly in silent death, and only an abiding nostalgia for the old North Country. Sandoz's perceptions of Native realities underwent a significant change during the arc of her writing career, and she sought to enlighten the American public of these changing realities as well. In April 1954, she published a short article in *Family Weekly* entitled "The Indian Looks at His Future"—perhaps a surprise for many Americans who believed all Indians to be dead or locked away on distant reservations waiting to die.[17] In the article, she makes plain that Native peoples have not vanished and are planning for the eventualities of the coming time.

Increasing Activism

Advocacy for American Indians did not just entail writing a few letters to legislators, however. Sandoz became involved with a group of forward thinking non-Indians who cared deeply for the tribes' subjection to stringent governmental policies. The Association on American Indian Affairs (AAIA) was composed of a wide assortment of influential people—some famous, some not—who focused on assisting the tribes in seven focused areas: education, health, land tenure, industry, irrigation, religion, and autonomy. The group was originally formed in 1922, but became seriously fragmented; then in the late 1930s, Pulitzer Prize-winning novelist Oliver LaFarge, author of *Laughing Boy* (1929), became chairman, and the regional Native rights groups merged into one.[18] Sandoz began her affiliation with AAIA in 1950, alongside such notables as Angie Debo, Bernard DeVoto, Douglas Fairbanks, Will Rogers, Jr., (son of the great Cherokee humorist and social critic), and Eric Sevareid, among others. Though the New York-based association was not without some problems, historian Donald L. Fixico (Shawnee/Muscogee/Seminole) points to this group as one of the most adamant and vocal proponents for Native American rights during the termination years.[19] Sandoz remained a contributing member of the association for several years, though she refused an appointment to the board of directors. She believed herself unqualified and stated that her writing career was too demanding to dedicate the time she felt would be necessary to be a board member; she did, however, keep in touch with the organization into the 1960s. Although founded by non-Natives in the early twentieth century, the AAIA is now directed by American Indians themselves, and since 1995 is based out of South Dakota. The association's extensive archival collection is located in the Princeton University Library.

In addition to her correspondence campaign with Capitol Hill and her involvement with AAIA, Sandoz also often made the journey to Washington, D.C., to speak personally with politicians who could assist or intercede on behalf of Native Americans. A savvy judge of character, Sandoz ferreted out the powerful people who had a hand in legislation that could affect the tribes. After scouting the political terrain, she would then recommend the political allies and connections to the tribal representatives, such as Northern Cheyenne chairman Rufus Wallowing. Wallowing, in turn, could then speak with these politicians on subsequent visits to the nation's capitol as a tribal delegate. Sandoz and Wallowing formed an enduring friendship, exchanging correspondence and personal visits (both in Montana and New York City) with one another until the end of her life.

Chapter Three focuses on Sandoz's letters criticizing the negative stereotyping so prevalent in American cinema and popular fiction during the 1940s through the 1960s. Sandoz was well aware that few people in the American mainstream cared about or even thought about American Indians other than as relics of the past. Most Americans of all backgrounds—even some Indians themselves—were steeped in the rampant racial stereotypes omnipresent in American culture. This concerned her deeply and she took great strides toward setting the record straight on this issue. The new medium of television was also guilty of promoting negative images of "the savage Indian," and Sandoz realized early on the broad impact television could wield. As the letters will show, she tried to combat the distortions of Native Americans whenever she encountered them in books, paintings, or in movies. It is not surprising that the sharpest and most scathing missives are written in regard to films based loosely on her books, *Crazy Horse* and *Cheyenne Autumn*. In 1954, the production of *Chief Crazy Horse*, starring Victor Mature as Crazy Horse, came to theatres; then ten years later came John Ford's *Cheyenne Autumn*, with a cumbersome cast of Hollywood notables, but little to do with the actual book. Sandoz hated them both and had no qualms about voicing her opinions as the correspondence reveals; far from delicate or gentle on this matter, her discourse is intensely direct and forceful. She thought both films contained blatant libels that were actionable, but she never pursued litigation for her own interests. In the end, she decided that *Chief Crazy Horse* was so horrific that she did not want her name connected to the film at all, even in a lawsuit. In several instances, her utter disgust with Hollywood's portrayal of American Indian people is palatable and not just where her books are concerned. One example is a brief, terse letter in 1954 to W. R. Frank Productions, the company responsible for producing a film on the life of Hunkpapa leader and holy man, Sitting Bull. Sandoz gets straight to the point: "No wonder so few pictures based on American Indians are worth seeing"; she writes, "a picture on this great Indian leader can be a very tremendous success . . . but not if it is falsified even to the background."[20]

Chapter Four addresses perhaps the most intriguing aspect about Sandoz: that of her advocacy for Native artists and writers; plus her promotion of education for and about American Indians. This part of her life has not yet been thoroughly explored; but it is perhaps the most interesting, for it speaks to her concerns that Native people be listened to and have their work appreciated. Sandoz possessed a complex personality—many times she has been described as prickly and difficult to deal with; but in this section her letters reveal a generous woman who was intensely concerned that American Indians become successful as writers and artists. Through good writing and artistic endeavor, Sandoz believed that American Indians could truly speak to the dominant culture and their own, and perhaps tear down oppressive barriers that had been in place for far too long. Sandoz had battled hard for her own rhetorical sovereignty with publishers and she knew if Native people could attain a degree of power over their own stories, perhaps a shift in perceptions of Native Americans could come to pass.

Commitment to Native Americans Past and Present

Sandoz's interest in Native American culture and history never waned; even in her last days as she was dying from terminal cancer she worked as best she could on final projects, including the completion of an introduction for Blish's *A Pictographic History of the Oglala Sioux*, and the writing of *The Battle of the Little Bighorn*. Her version of that particular battle was quite critical of George Armstrong Custer and the governmental policy of American Indian extermination that he represented. She took this stance even during the time when many American writers still cast him as heroic. Sandoz realized as few writers did before her how important Native American history was to American history in general—that American Indian history was *essential* to the study of American history—and she was committed to sharing that knowledge, as these letters will show. The correspondence also illustrates Sandoz's commitment to Native American self-determination and tribal sovereignty, and points out the various ways she allied herself to the tribes in their political struggles. Activist, ally, advocate—all these are descriptors of Mari Sandoz in connection with American Indians—character traits that reveal themselves in her books, and most clearly in the letters she penned from the 1940s through the 1960s.

I Do Not Apologize

1.
Quest
for
Historical
Accuracy

E   ven though Mari Sandoz always thought of herself primarily as a historian, and her research methodologies were quite competent and meticulous, it is important to remember that she was not a degreed academic historian. Nevertheless, she held herself to specific standards of historical accuracy that she had studied during her years at the University of Nebraska and in her work at the Nebraska Historical Society. Her training in historical research was largely motivated by her interest in getting at the truth, and came to fruition under the influence and tutelage of professors Fred Morrow Fling and John D. Hicks at the University of Nebraska–Lincoln. Sandoz always used the elaborate filing systems developed by Dr. Fling, who advocated using primary sources and careful scrutiny of evidence. He was also known for his "balanced and multi-disciplinary approach to historical issues, but his personality was mercurial and autocratic," according to Sandoz scholar Richard Voorhees.[1] Interestingly, in some respects, Fling's personality may have had significant similarities to that of Sandoz's father, Jules, who certainly fit the description of an autocrat. Whatever the case, Fling's system for organizing and indexing source materials and his insistence on historical fact influenced Sandoz for her entire career. Professor Hicks, on the other hand, began teaching at the university in the early 1920s, near the time that Sandoz first arrived in Lincoln from the Sandhills. Because her attendance at UNL was dictated by time and finances, Sandoz did not become his student until 1932.[2] It was most likely her experience of his American Frontier history course which confirmed for her that writing about her region, its peoples, and its history was a worthwhile task. Hicks, less volatile than Professor Fling, may have been more approachable; it is clear from Sandoz's letter to the Atlantic Press in 1932 regarding *Old Jules* that she admired

Professor Hicks greatly.[3] Like Fling, he promoted a more interdisciplinary approach to the study of history. Also, Hicks's methodology was more in line with the writing that Sandoz was already engaged in—that of "writing what you know."[4]

Additionally, Sandoz's position as a research assistant at the Nebraska State Historical Society (NSHS) for Dr. Addison Sheldon gave her valuable experience working with archival materials. While Fling and Hicks certainly influenced her sense of historical theory and methods, the experience and practice she gained at the NSHS, and the wealth of materials available to her there, left an indelible impression on her, her writing, and her research methodology as well. Of particular interest to Sandoz were newspaper accounts and firsthand accounts (diaries and interviews) of early events involving Indian and white relationships and encounters. She and Sheldon, both of whom were interested in primary sources regarding the history of Native Americans of the Great Plains, remained friends and correspondents for many years. The first letter in this chapter, in fact, is to Sheldon regarding historical military records and notes pertaining to Chief Red Cloud. No doubt Sandoz developed an affinity for digging through archives and repositories of historical collections from her early work at NSHS. Sandoz certainly possessed a viable amount of scholarly historical training and practical experience with documents, yet she is still considered by many to be unorthodox as a historian.

It is equally pertinent to remember that, in the main, Sandoz was a storyteller, one who would often include fictional elements in her "nonfiction" historical works; for example, she often used invented scenes or dialogue for dramatic effect, and sometimes invented characters to move the action along. These elements were always employed with a high degree of verisimilitude; however, professional historians and literary critics would lambaste her on these issues throughout her writing career. Undeterred, she most often dismissed those critics and defended her work as authentic. Many scholars still take issue with this aspect of her writing, and reject her work as inconsequential or fraudulent, but I would argue to the contrary. Sandoz grew up in a unique atmosphere—even though she was a child living out in the remote regions of the Great Plains, it nevertheless was (and still is) a cross-roads, an intersection of history and literature. She came of age amid dramatic storytellers and makers of history, and Sandoz learned early on that there were various versions of "histories." Surely this situation piqued her intense curiosity that later revealed itself in her drive to "get at the truth." But the story intrigued her equally—and not just for the entertainment it provid-

Mari Sandoz and (probably) Eleanor Hinman in front of the Model T in which they journeyed to Pine Ridge, 1930. Caroline Sandoz Pifer Collection, Mari Sandoz High Plains Heritage Center—Chadron State College. 2003.001.00312.

ed. Sandoz was keenly aware of the lessons a good story could impart to the audience. Likewise, the oral histories she heard as a youngster were told by men and women who had lived them; these she judged to have validity, if not documentation. For Sandoz, the truth was in the stories, and that philosophy never really left her. She knew and drew on a wide array of literacies for her writing and research. Perhaps this is why, in some ways, Sandoz's writing could be termed "genre fusion," "genre defiant," or "hybrid text," as she often blended the real and the imagined in her work. It is clear that it stood apart from the accepted literary categorization in its day, and in many respects still stands apart today. Others might characterize her historical writings as "embroidered" or "accessorized," but whatever the case, Sandoz strove systematically to ground all her nonfiction in solid historical research. Stauffer points out that although many authors of Western writing do not always give credit to Sandoz, they still draw upon her material as *bona fide*:

Sometimes Sandoz's material—great swatches of it—can be found embedded unacknowledged in someone else's book. Two recent publications about the Midwestern states owe her credit for their information about Crazy Horse, for instance. Authors have been known to insert smaller extracts of her material into their work, apparently willing to accept her information but unwilling to credit her as a source.[5]

It is, in fact, Sandoz's nonfiction and Indian writings that draw the most attention and that are generally recognized as her greatest achievement. Two books in particular, *Crazy Horse* and *Cheyenne Autumn,* have long been favorites of both American Indian and non-Indian readers. Both books have seen several reprints and are still in production with University of Nebraska Press's Bison Books; and *Crazy Horse* was chosen as the state of Nebraska's "One Book" in 2007. These books are remarkable because within them the reader comes to realize that Sandoz didn't just sympathize with American Indians, she appreciated them and their contributions to the history of the nation. She wanted those contributions to be known; she wanted Native American histories and stories to be appreciated and understood as integral to the history of the United States. As the letters will show, Sandoz went to great lengths to find and present history as accurately as possible and most often relied on primary sources for her facts.

The letters in this section are an interesting array of missives, pointing out the ways Sandoz went about gathering historical information, as well as correcting misconceptions about American Indians. As the reader will see, the letters often contain miniature history lessons in themselves, as Sandoz seldom turned down a chance to share knowledge. It is also clear that Sandoz sometimes worked through her ideas in the letters themselves, ideas that would later turn up in her other writings. For example, in a letter to Edward Weeks, her editor at Atlantic Press, she includes extended descriptions that will later be found in *Cheyenne Autumn*; she closes with the statement, "I am sorry to ramble on so, but it's important to get these impressions down in rough shape, so you suffer."[6] Many of the letters here contain great details and explanations of significant cultural import.

Additionally, one will note that Sandoz corresponds and networks with others engaged in the writing of history, offering encouragement or paths to further source materials. Sandoz was well acquainted with many of the repositories and historical archives in several regions. She traveled extensively to do research all across the Great Plains states from Texas up to Montana; and in the East she worked in libraries and archives in New York City, and

Mari Sandoz in one of her New York apartments with manuscripts and papers on table. Caroline Sandoz Pifer Collection, Mari Sandoz High Plains Heritage Center—Chadron State College. 2003.001.00068.

most often in Washington, D.C. While most of the data she retrieved is pre-served in her vast note-card index and various papers housed in the Sandoz Collection, a great deal of the information she gathered finds its way into portions of the correspondence. As Sandoz biographer Stauffer points out, it seems clear that Sandoz knew her correspondence would one day be of interest to other researchers.[7] That Sandoz would so carefully preserve such a large volume of letters speaks to this as well—it must have been a difficult enterprise to find safe storage for such a collection over the years. As Mari would say, "But enough—"; it is time for us to consider her words.

Dr. A.E. Sheldon
Nebraska State Historical Society,
Lincoln, Nebraska

Dear Doctor:

I put off answering your queries and those of Miss Poast until the end
of my snoop through the archives, as the material from the Indian Bureau
and the War Department was moved in so recently that no one is very
certain just what is there, and any day my nose might lead me to something
important.

Now, in looking back upon the five very busy weeks there (I took no
time to call anyone, not even Ruth—I worked until ten every night) I have
this incomplete report to make.

BUREAU OF INDIAN AFFAIRS

I took up the matter of a possible index with the proper people and discovered that all they have is the common topical organization. The Indian
material is in file like this:

Commissions
Com of Indian Affairs
Inspector
Superintendencies Agencies, etc.

with the various offices represented, if the records are complete, by Letter
Books, sent and received, and the document files, including the telegrams,
letters, vouchers, etc. sent to that particular office. The document files of
the Commissioner are separated into agencies of origin and are arranged
alphabetically. From the files pertaining to Red Cloud, material on certain
subjects has been collected into special files, such as the Marsh investigation. I found, however, that this was not well and thoroughly done and
the only way to be sure that everything on a given subject had been seen is
to go through every one pertaining to the period. Another complicating
factor is the apparent disappearance of so many documents. The official de-
scriptive jacket is there, but the documents have been removed, very often
without any memo of time, purpose, or place. [. . .]

MILITARY RECORDS

These are collected by post, expedition, department, military division
and War Department. The material of the 1870s, from the Division of the

Missouri, contains many special files, such as "Sioux War of 1876," "Little Wolf Papers," etc. Again, the collecting was sketchy, and I found some most important material loose among the mess of petty administrative detail papers. The researcher in the War Archives labors under another handicap: large files, like those of the Black Hills Expedition of 1876 [1874?] for example have not yet been located and all that is available in these cases is the other end of the correspondence. The Fort Robinson material is still at the post, but they write me from there that 1876–77 is missing. No one seems to know if these records were ordered to Washington or someplace else for one of the endless investigations of the period and lost—or if they are still among the piles of material not yet unboxed at the archives. (The war records were moved very recently, some in 1940.)

IDENTIFICATION OF PUBLISHED MATERIAL

Apparently the researcher is left to discover by actual comparison with the documents whether any given one has been published. A common practice seems to have been to publish a letter or report in the condensed form transmitted to higher offices rather than in the full version. About the Grattan Affair: I suspect that all the material in the special file has been well pawed over, if not published. Until the archives are really organized, the new material on such famous incidents will probably be that which the determined and lucky researcher turns up in unexpected places. The above seems to hold true for the Twiss material and any other. The descendants of Twiss, incidentally, seem to be called Twist, as you may have discovered.

About the Richard tribe: I'm familiar with the outfit. Old Jules knew several of them and always compared them unfavorably to the Cuneys and the Ecoffeys. Evidently the earlier Richards were mixed up in a lot of frontier activities besides running bridges and ferries, such as the liquor trade, hijacking freighting outfits, etc. A couple of the younger ones killed the two sons of Antoine Janis in a drunken brawl Christmas day in Nick Janis' camp near the Sod Agency. Antoine was on the Republican with Little Wound's band and came up to take the bodies of these sons to Laramie, where you saw the graves. John (who was supposed to have killed a soldier at Fetterman fled north to Red Cloud and was granted forgiveness for bringing the chief in) was killed in Yellow Bear's tipi on the Platte, the old man Richard on the Niobrara with one of the Palladays. [. . .]

I am enclosing some notes on the Sod Agency for you. The [plate] of the place is coming from Washington in a week or so. Of particular interest are Smith's reports about the agency as he found it when he was commanding officer of Ft. Laramie, took it over temporarily in 1871. Many of these citations, particularly the ones that seemed of special interest, I took with the actual document number so if you want to have the original Photostatted, done at cost by the archives, you can send in for the whole thing. I looked at every document in the Red Cloud files for 1871 to the removal of the Cheyennes, May 1877, and if you find any point upon which you think I might have discovered something special that I might overlook as being unimportant to you, tell me and I'll be glad to search my notes. I covered better than a ream of sheets with very condensed writing, both sides, so I must have stumbled upon something. The War Department Records were, in many cases, stuck tightly together with old rubber bands, said to be put on over fifty years ago. Whole files had not been looked into since, chiefly, I suspect, they were store[d] in garrets and basements and not available.

Sincerely,

———

JUNE 25, 1940

Mr. Charles Nines[8]
Burroughs Adding Machine Co.

Detroit, Michigan

Dear Charlie Nines:

[. . .] The last few years I've been working on two Indian biographies, a Cheyenne and a Sioux, and every once in a while I run across the Nines name, particularly in the material collected by Judge Ricker of Chadron. George Wilson tells me you did the interviewing for the American museum [during the] summers. All together you must have a lot of information tucked away in your head about Reservation characters that interest me, such as Red Cloud and his followers, including American Horse, the Goings family, Spider, Red Dog, Woman's Dress, etc. and the Young Man Afraid of His Horse crowd, the No Water camp, Little Big Man, etc. Did you know Big Bat, Billy Garnett or Hunter, and old Frank Salaway?

I know all these questions would be an imposition to anyone but a Nebraska Panhandlite. I am banking on your good nature and that you are still one of us.

Sincerely,

———

I Do Not Apologize

NOVEMBER 22, 1940

Mrs. Bettelyoun[9]
Soldier and Sailors Home
Hot Springs, South Dakota

Dear Mrs. Bettelyoun:

Business compelled me to hurry back to Denver from my speaking engagements down in Nebraska in September so I couldn't come up to Hot Springs then. Now I'm planning to go to Cheyenne within the next two weeks and if I can see you then I hope to come on to Hot Springs.

My plans are three-fold. I'm making a final checkup in the Historical Society here [in Denver] and in Cheyenne for my story of Dull Knife and for Dr. Sheldon's compilation of material on Red Cloud. Then there's my eagerness to collect and preserve all historical material for the future, and, even more important just now, ever since I read your story, I've wanted to go over it with you, to stimulate you to recall more details, more of the life of the times. If you haven't [had] your story published yet, I'd like very much to go over your story with you. You have priceless material and my interest in the preservation of the history of the West and its presentation to the public makes me anxious to see that you make the most of your recollections. If you would like to talk the story over with me, I shall bring my portable typewriter with me and make notes for you as we go.

In return for this I would like to have you help us on a few things from your memory of Dull Knife and some things of Red Cloud's family connections, which as you will know, are pretty confused. I haven't had a vacation this year and so if it takes a week, or even longer to do this, I will be happy to do it. I'm so interested in Indian history it will be great fun for me.

Please let me know if you can see me if I come.

Thank-you,

————

FEBRUARY 3, 1941

Knopf Publishers

Dear Paul:[10]
[. . .]
My own material is in much better shape than I dared hope and I may be able to put off the Washington interruption until towards fall, as a sort

of final check on the book, with the reservation junket first. I've quit the speechifying. Talked to the [Denver] Chamber of Commerce last week mainly to help head off the naming of a Denver street for Colonel Chivington, the fanatical Methodist minister who led the most shameful Indian massacre of American history. He with his troops fell upon a Cheyenne village called in by the Indian agent, butchered men, women, and children, brought in a whole mess of what are technically called "short hair" scalps, taken from the butchered Cheyenne women, showed them around town here. Of course I didn't mention this part, but I didn't need to; the battle had been won by the various historians around town. I had a grand time exposing a few frontier bad men and went home. [. . .]

The cuts of the Shoshone canyon came from my old file of local pictures for the Indian books. Obviously these are too modern for a feel of the setting. Look at them and be homesick, and throw away.

Affectionately,

———

JUNE 16, 1941

Helen Blish
2441 Sheridan Ave.
Detroit, Michigan

Dear Helen:
[. . .]
I don't know whether Eleanor told you that she relinquished her priority right on Crazy Horse to me. She did it as a complete surprise to me, with her typical generosity and graciousness. I intend to dedicate the book to her, if she'll let me, after she's got some indication of what I am making of her beloved subject. I hope it won't disappoint her too much. The book has to be in Knopf's hands March 1, 1942, so I'm putting it together now. The story is tremendous, with all the cumulative inevitability of Greek tragedy, and I feel small and mean and incompetent, although I've done my best to get at the truth. If I can only pin it down on paper.

In the meantime there are still some points that I'd like to talk over with you and Eleanor. After over a year of intensive work on the material and a couple months in Washington in the archives, there are still gaps, discrepancies and contradictions and what look like deliberate evasions and omissions, particularly in the family relationships. These are due, partly at least, I suspect, to the deep and permanent animosities of the old feud

I Do Not Apologize

between the Smoke and Bear people, both in the early period and in the agency days, when most of the accounts got into print and into manuscript. To aggravate these animosities, there were all the later contributory splits, such as the killing of Grattan, the breed feuds, as that between the Janis and Richard factions, up to the killing of Crazy Horse himself, and the aftermath. I'm going to Pine Ridge after I get done at the Writer's Conference at Boulder, along in August, mostly for the Indian feel. Apparently, the more reliable and the more communicative sources have died. Perhaps I can get at the family relationships that Nick Janis once worked out for the agency. Anyway, I suspect that by now you and Eleanor are better sources . . . so I'd like to get at you with my relationship files—they're pretty fat and revealing and still full of holes. If I don't manage to inveigle you into my web before, may I come through Detroit sometime this fall with the file?

[. . .]

Sincerely,

———

OCTOBER 8, 1941

Eleanor Hinman

Dear Eli:

It was fine to see you again, and you're well to go to so much trouble for me, particularly when you have your own work in progress. I am, of course, very pleased to have your approval of the dedication but if you find yourself weakening again, don't hesitate to say so, for despite all my anxiety to give you some credit for your work, your generosity, and your kindness, I won't make you unhappy about it if I can help it.

Now about the notes you so generously got together: I don't think I can answer all your queries short of the whole written book, with a transcript of my notes all added, and perhaps not then, for the problem of tribal and band business is full of contradictions, and the points of erosion rival the Grand Canyon. I am fully convinced now that in the historic period prior to 1857–8, the Oglalas were a fluid outfit. It's not to be wondered at. They went through two great cultural upheavals in a period of not more than 150 years: from an approximately stone age, agrarian Indian about the Great Lakes to, first, an iron-armed horse-mounted buffalo hunter of the Plains, and then, before the first change had time to crystallize into a set pattern, they had to change into a white-infused, gun-armed resister of final white-man domination. During that time, I think that there was probably only one period in which the Oglala band were at all distinct—1857–1868, and the bands of that period seem to have cut across many of the older lines, or what passed for lines. Much of the leadership of the Oglalas seems to have been taken over, between 1840 and 1850, by Smoke and his cohorts, with the help of trader presents and the killing of Bull Bear—taken over by Smoke, who never claimed to be anything but a Saone and his nephew, Red Cloud, who was evidently a Brule-Saone. In 1857 Old Smoke was relegated to a lodge among the Loafers, part of the time at Deer Creek, the rest of the time at the woman's camp at Laramie. His son was nominally head of the band called by his nickname, or so it seems, and that band was already dominated by Red Cloud, while the old band that was formerly supposed to be Lone Man's [Red Cloud's father] was taken over by 1857 by the son of one of his sub-chiefs, Man Afraid. That means to me that Red Cloud may have had some difficulty in his early period with his band. Perhaps the fact that his father drank so much made it advisable that he practice the custom of the common man among the Sioux—go to his mother's people. Of course, he was orphaned very early.

About the name Hunkpatila: it doesn't seem to mean so much. There's considerable evidence that there was a Hunkpatila or Hunkpatina (meaning the same) in each of the Teton divisions. Even the Yanktonai had a Hunkpatina band, meaning to camp at the end of the circle. Man Afraid, according to He Dog, was a Minneconjou, according to Hyde, he was a Kyuska, according to other references he was a Saone. Probably, he was all of these, a Saone (because he was a Minne) on one side of the house and a Kyuska on the other and therefore a full-fledged latter day Oglala. The Cut-Offs are not the same as the Pushed Asides; Little Wound was made chief of the Cut-Offs in 1870.

Anyway, as soon as the Oglalas moved away from Laramie . . . Man Afraid is listed as a Hunkpatila and Little Hawk (Long Face according to my conclusions) as one of his sub-chiefs. In those days the Bad Faces were a distinct crowd, see He Dog for this. He Dog says he and Crazy Horse stayed with Man Afraid in the early period of their manhood. Later, this group divided and a new group was formed of which He Dog, Big Road, Black Twin and Red Cloud were joint Chiefs. What a nice suggestion of movement within the People there! He Dog must have shifted, or else Red Cloud did. I think there was a double-shift—that Red Cloud moved his Bad Faces farther up, that Sword and his outfit stayed down with Man Afraid, and He Dog went up with the Bad Faces. Then, not three years later, there must have been another shift, for apparently some of each of the earlier camps followed Red Cloud and Man Afraid in, and some of each camp stayed out.

After this the Oglalas that stayed out were called Crazy Horse Indians, both in the agency record and in the army reports. All the earlier band distinctions seem to have disappeared. Incidentally, Red Cloud did NOT live at the Sod Agency more than 2–3 weeks a year. He was usually at least as far out as Raw Hide Buttes, even in the winter, and sending runners every now and then complaining that his monthly issue wasn't fetched up to him. In the meantime such folk as Little Big Man and Big Road would appear on the agency roster for issue. It certainly makes a mad-house prospect of anyone who goes in for this business.

About Woman's Dress being an orphan—I think He Dog meant he was an Orphan, which was a band distinction that shows up among both the Brules and the Oglalas in early accounts and is made official by Hayden, 1862. This name was revived later for the descendants of men who went to Washington, Dorsey 1897. [. . .]

About this band business: From 1866 to 1868 every northern Oglala was a Bad Face because the popular hero, Red Cloud, was one. From 1868 he was a Crazy Horse Indian. I'm not worrying so much about the band as about the man they were following at any given time.

About the Thunder Cult of Crazy Horse: I know about it and I know how elusive the business is. It reminds me of the Horse Society, the one that died out leaving no one knowing much about it because only four men at a time belonged, and the membership was not renewed after the 1850s. Almost nothing was ever said publicly about either the secrets or the purposes of the organization. When I get the actual happenings nailed down, I shall try to go from the known to the unknown in such things. To work with two unknowns at one time is too much for my pale brain. [. . .]

About Iron Shield: It seems odd that with all the agency Indians, the breeds and the captives, including such people as Little Big Man, etc. and one of Red Cloud's daughters, that Anson Mills had to draw upon, there should be any dispute about the name of the man shot through the bowels at Slim Buttes. All the AGO records, including those of the Military Division of the Missouri, the Department of the Platte, Fort Laramie Letter books and Fort Robinson reports, and all the personal reports of such officers as Crook, Mills, and all Mills' subordinate officers, give the name as American Horse. Surely Grouard, Little Bat, Stirk, (who married Little Bat's sister) and Little Big Man, etc., couldn't all have been mistaken. However, I've already established the practice of giving both names when there is a dispute.

[. . .]

Affectionately,

———

OCTOBER 24, 1942

Stuart Rose

Dear Stuart Rose:

Your very kind letters about the early version of *Crazy Horse* have gone unanswered an appallingly long time. I regret things like that very much but it seems I either write or write letters, never both.

However, the book is now through the production difficulties, off the press November 2, with publication November 30. When this was announced my telephone was put to a great deal of unpatriotic use. I hadn't realized how many people still have strong feelings about the Sioux wars, pro and con; people from as far away as Ohio called. Three strangers in rapid succession demanded to know whether I had decided Sitting Bull was really a coward at the Custer battle and let Crazy Horse and Gall fight the soldiers alone. I'll admit that I had worked with the material so long that I forgot about such minor whiteman controversies.

But the questions did remind me of the material for the enclosed story, "The Giveaway." When Crazy Horse was killed the northern Oglalas, all except Little Big Man, watched for their opportunity to slip away north to Sitting Bull and when they came back there were quite a few women leaders among the surrendering Sioux (so many of the prominent men were lost during those trying times). The 4th Annual Report, Bureau of Ethnology, lists four women band leaders in Big Road's Oglalas alone.

From my childhood and my later contacts with the Pine Ridge Reservation I recall many fine stories of these women, stories that made the commonly accepted white man's notion of the Sioux woman as a drudge seem pretty absurd.

I hope I got a little of this feeling into the story.

Sincerely,

———

MARCH 9, 1943

Judge Louis Lightener

Dear Judge:

Thank you for the fine letter about *Crazy Horse*. It was a tremendous undertaking and I am glad that I did not fail too miserably.

About the discrepancies between my book and many printed sources: There are two main reasons for this besides the obvious one that I might be mistaken. First, there is a great deal of misinformation floating around in print and second, the truth was buried in the war department archives and not available until 1940.

As you know, most of the Indian stories of the past were based upon newspaper reports and neither you nor I would regard [them] as reliable. Besides, there was the propaganda value of atrocity stories—the method always used to justify expropriation of a people. Even the accounts of General Miles and General Dodge are unreliable. Miles' book was written by a ghost writer, as is admitted, obliquely, in the foreword, and when I started checking it against the General's signed reports to his superiors at the time of the Sioux wars, there was just almost no ground for comparison. The personal account was fictional. General Dodge's book is completely discredited. It is an appalling collection of atrocity stories and Ned Buntline type of history, and repeated and quoted by frontier writers who wanted to write the truth but had neither the time or the opportunity (or training) to question it or disprove it.

All this time the war department archives were in basements, attics, and warehouses all over Washington, the frontier records mostly in big bales tied up with cord or mule rope just as they came in [when] the posts were closed. There was no check list of what these bundles contained and no staff to watch researchers and so the material was almost literally unavailable to anyone. I broke the war department down by patient sitting in the front office and because I found someone there who had read *Old Jules* and remembered Dr. Walter Reed. The sight of the material, subject to complete destruction from one match appalled me so that I raised my voice all over Washington, including an outburst at the dinner table of Senator Norris. It was a rude, unmannerly outburst, but the Senator was interested, said there was some agitation for a National Archives building; perhaps it should be hastened. So, by 1940 the stuff was being brought in to fire proof shelvings in a fire proof building. By now, when the war restrictions are off, in the future it will be easy to prove such points as that Custer's hair was cut off before he went on the 1876 campaign. I saw the order. Of course I knew about this before from the Indians and from the protests of the old timers in the papers when the beer company's painting showed up in the saloons. The soldiers carried no swords that day either—frontier troops hadn't for some time.

But enough about that. I agree with you about the who's who of the Indians in the book. But it would have meant including a whole "binder" that should be at least 8 pages more to get the one page in, so I didn't get any encouragement from the publisher on that. Unfortunately, the author has little to say about a book's make-up.

[. . .]

Sincerely,

———

MARCH 25, 1943

Mr. George Philip
United States Attorney,
Rapid City, South Dakota

Dear Mr. Philip

[. . .]

I know why so many people dropped the Crazy Horse story—it is a tremendous undertaking. Just the index to my notes required 15,000 cards and even so, I'm sure to have made the wrong decision on some of the controversial issues, but I did my damndest. You would have been a good one to do the story.

About the questions you ask: No, I don't know where Crazy Horse was finally laid. The Indians told me that he was buried several places, first temporarily in some bluffs, then carried north towards the Yellow Medicine, for they had to go when their champion was gone, and then several later places. A few years ago some Indian wrote the Nebraska State Historical Society offering them Crazy Horse's remains in exchange, I think, for a Model T. I doubt if anyone could identify the actual spot by this time, which is perhaps somewhere up near Manderson. Not that I think it matters. His proper place in the annals of the great, it seems to me, and his story has a special and peculiar pertinency just now, when thoughtful people are considering the protection of the minorities of the world.

About the Larrabee woman: The Indians said she left when the troubles started, evidently before He Dog moved across the creek. What probably happened was that she knew so much of what was coming that she indicated her uneasiness and was told by Crazy Horse to return to her mother until the trouble was over. That would be the probable procedure, and without any suggestion of hard feelings or disloyalty she could go. Some of the more sentimental women around the agency, mostly white women, have written me that they think I was too easy on her and on Black Buffalo Woman both—that they were deserting their men in troubled times. They

I Do Not Apologize

don't understand the Indian point of view. In troubled times it is better to have the women with their own people. I have some actual items on this in my notes, but they are in storage in Denver. The Larrabee woman's name is variously given, sometimes Nellie. One of the Ricker interviews speaks of her and her sister as very pretty girls, evidently with some schooling. She bore Crazy Horse no child so far as any source indicates. I have several references for her marriage to Crazy Horse #2, as the Indians began to call him, and he is the one listed on the annuity rolls. If she had any children they seem to have dropped out of sight. "Everybody is dead" He Dog said in 1930, adding that some of the No Water people still lived, sons of descendants of sons. [. . .]

Sincerely,

———

SEPTEMBER 7, 1945

Mr. Don Russell
The Chicago Daily News
Chicago, Illinois

Dear Mr. Russell:

Returning from a summer in Colorado, I find several notes about your letter to the Phoenix West, *Saturday Review of Literature*, regarding my interest in the killing of Yellow Hand. Evidently the monument referred to in the articles you cite was the one dedicated September 9, 1934, at Montrose, Nebraska, to Col. Wesley Merritt and the Fifth Cavalry for the interception of the 800 Cheyenne and Sioux en route to join the hostiles in the north, July 17, 1876. If you are interested in this dedication you will find a report of it in the *Nebraska History Magazine*, Vol. IV No.2. I was director of research at the Nebraska State Historical Society at the time as well as associate editor of the magazine and it was my responsibility to correct and approve the wording on the plaque for the monument and to organize the day's formalities and speaking.

The Society spent considerable time the year preceding the dedication trying to verify the Captain King story of the killing of Yellow Hand. The findings gave Dr. A.E. Sheldon, superintendent of the Society (and a newspaperman at Chadron, 1889–1899) no choice; he had to deny Mrs. Johnny Baker's suggestion that Buffalo Bill's name go on the plaque. Instead, she put up another monument a few rods away, without either Dr. Sheldon or Chris Madsen speaking there.

Prior to 1934, Dr. Sheldon and I had both carried on years of correspondence with Chris Madsen about the Sioux war of 1876. Never during all this correspondence, or during the talks before, or during the dedication, or at any time since have I ever heard Mr. Madsen deviate from his story that Buffalo Bill had nothing to do with the killing of Yellow Hand. Certainly none of the 800 Indians on the Warbonnet that day thought so or Cody's life would have been mighty uneasy. As his partner, Captain Luther North told me, the Indians protected Bill's cattle from the northern raiders and made his beaded show costumes. I've heard Cody himself tell at our dinner table how the Cheyennes had carried him home when they found him drunk on the prairie. Never did I hear him say a word about killing an Indian.

But, all this is foolishness. My purpose in running down such stories goes beyond my interest in the truth. What I am trying to do is to show that the technique for expropriating a minority is the same everywhere, in all times. Once the Sioux and the Cheyennes were a romantic, wondrous people, to be visited by foreign princes and lords and by sick and unhappy writers from Boston. Then came the time when the majority wanted their land, so they were made out as subhuman, as beasts, and men who killed them, or said they did, became heroes.

Sincerely,

————

OCTOBER 24, 1945

The Frontier Press Company
505 Fifth Avenue,
New York City

Gentlemen:

On the strength of a call from one of your representatives who was checking up on me as a purchaser of the *Lincoln Library*, I am taking the liberty to point out a bit of misinformation in the volume.

On page 514, bottom, second column:

One cannot speak of the Sioux and Dakotas as parallels, any more than one can say coal and anthracite that way. The Dakotas are a division of the Sioux, as the whiteman calls the Dakota-Lakota Indians. The western section has no "D" in their language, and so call themselves Lakotas.

Geographically, your distribution of Indians in the Mississippi Valley is not good, you have only the Northeast, East and center occupied. In historical times the Dakotas lived in the Minnesota, upper Missouri river regions; the Lakotas west and southwest of them, in what are now the Dakotas and all along the high Plains north of the Arkansas river to beyond the Milk in Montana. Corn growing Indians lived as far west as the 100th meridian and farther. The corn growers were, of course, village dwellers, with earth (Omaha, Ponca, Pawnee, Otoe, etc.) or grass (Wichita) houses. For a clear picture of this region I refer you to the readily available authority, *Handbook of American Indians*, Bureau of American Ethnology Publications.

In your biographies:

Sitting Bull was not in the massacre of 1862. He was a Hunkpapa of the Teton, the western, nomadic buffalo-hunting Sioux, the Lakota, who were peaceful in 1862. The massacre of 1862 was 700–800 miles east of Sitting Bull; the participants were Dakotas, led by Little Crow and Inkpaduta. [. . .].

Nor was Bill Cody a member of the Nebraska Legislature. See a list of the Nebraska legislative members or Watkins' or Sheldon's history of Nebraska. I know that he claimed he was, in *Who's Who*, but a few other whoppers have found their way between those red covers.

Sorry, but I do keep hoping that someday some compiler will stop to do a little checking on western source material, and not keep perpetuating the same old canards and misconceptions.

Sincerely,

————

AUGUST 29, 1948

T.V. Flannery
81 Robin Street
Albany, New York

Dear Mr. Flannery:

Forgive the delay in my reply to your note about a picture of Crazy Horse. My brother Jules forwarded it promptly from Gordon, Nebraska, but I was away at the University of Wisconsin, where I had charge of the advanced work in the Writers Institute.

No, the Wayne picture in the March *Holiday*, 1945, is not Crazy Horse, the Oglala war leader. It couldn't be even a Teton Lakota; the accouterments are wrong. I've seen this picture before, perhaps have it in my Indian material in storage at Denver since the beginning of the war. Anyway, I guess that man to be of some Missouri River tribe. Certainly not Crazy Horse.

I know of no picture of the Oglala war chief. I've been on the lookout for one all my life. I heard He Dog say over the spread of 30 years that none was ever taken and, after looking through every likely repository from here to Utah, and the dozens of pictures offered every year to the Nebraska State Historical Society (and now to me), I am convinced He Dog and his brother, Short Bull were right. There is no picture.

Of course there was C.H. #2, as the Indians called him; Greasy Head, who married a Crazy Horse widow and took his illustrious predecessor's name, as you will know, was often done among the Lakotas. This picture was sold everywhere on postcards—a dark little man in a warbonnet. There is another Crazy Horse, a Blood Indian, but his picture couldn't be mistaken for the Oglala. All those of the Blood Indian I've seen are of an old man.

I do have three sketches of Crazy Horse: two are done by Amos Bad Heart Bull, son of the historian of the Crazy Horse band, who was the uncle. These are in the two part folio called Sioux Paintings printed in Nice, France, which you probably have. The Amos Bad Heart Bull pictures, an entire account book of them are at the Carnegie foundation with the Helen Blish manuscript interpreting them. The Sioux folio pictures are from these. The best one I have is of the Reno fight sequence, with Crazy Horse in the center stripped to the breech cloth on his spotted yellow and white horse. The features are typically styled but the body has the hailstone spots of his medicine. The other is less distinguishable. The third I have is a painting of Crazy Horse and He Dog, charging their horses at a green mountain, the Black Hills, defending them. This is from a Crazy Horse Sacred Medicine Lodge.

Now you know all I do about this business—But it's important to those of us who like the truth, as you obviously do.

Sincerely,

———

SEPTEMBER 1, 1948

Maurice Frink
The Elkhart Truth
Elkhart, Indiana

Dear Maurice Frink:
Thank you for sending me the "Custer Controversy" in the *Denver Post*. I'm happy that some of these things are reaching print, and that you and Captain Luce are still busy—

I Do Not Apologize

I wonder if the Captain has a copy of the Amos Bad Heart Bull picture history of the Hostile Oglalas, which includes the Reno and Custer fights. The Carnegie Foundation gave Helen Blish a two year grant and a car for her work getting further interpretation of this thick account book of pictures after she got her master's degree on it at the University of Nebraska, where I saw it and spent much time over it, as well as her typescript later. With the grant Miss Blish went all over the Sioux reservations, and to the Cheyennes too, and then all the battle sites, etc. Perhaps you've seen the manuscript or the photographic reproductions and the typescript. There are five or six in existence, at least. One of these is here in the Clark Wissler material, I am told. I wish the Carnegie people would publish this. A little pressure would help, I think.

We took the maps from this work and a dozen or so more from the Indians, including He Dog's, along with these available from the white sources when we went to the Battlefield in 1930. We pitched our tent on the last little knob where Crazy Horse apparently circled around behind Custer. From there we went all over the ground, trying to follow the possible lines of approach of the reported groups of Indians, and then down over the route that was apparently followed by the officer Bad Heart Bull shows fleeing alone with several warriors in pursuit, the man's pistol turned upon himself, the explosion marked in the characteristic tufted spray of dark lines into his face. Going over this reminds me of the line dropped out by the printers from the scene in my *Crazy Horse.*

I've always felt that the battle must have been a moving one. That was always the picture the Indians gave as they sat around and drew the ground plat in the dust down on the river for my father and is certainly the story as we got it from the Indian accounts. Since the Indians usually picture a fight as they saw it, individually or as a group, one must, I suppose, put them together and plan [?] from that. There were the scattering of Cheyennes that charged up from between the Minneconjou and Hunkpapa camps, Gall, and as I recall, Crow King swinging off from the Reno fight with their warriors, cutting in towards the rear, rolling it up, while the Minneconjous and Oglalas were cutting in on the forward line of march considerably before the site of the last stand.

This has been a busy Crazy Horse summer, until my files are bursting with communications. [. . .]

Sincerely,

———

Mr. H. D. Wimer
Stratton, Nebraska

Dear Mr. Wimer:

Thank you for your fine, generous letter. Yes, I'm back on my Cheyenne book. I laid it aside, after three years of research, including four months in Washington in the AGO records and the Indian Bureau archives. I had uncovered much material that has not been available to anyone in the past on the Cheyenne difficulties.

Much of the last year I have been concentrating on the Oklahoma, Kansas, and Nebraska and Wyoming material that has reached publication since 1940, and all that has accumulated in the historical repositories these last few years. The index just to my notes has passed 30,000 cards, so there is probably little in print anywhere that has escaped my attention. But I'm anxious that nothing be overlooked. I want the whole story.

For all my voluminous material, there are still a few holes, particularly on the Indian blood relationships, such as just how closely related were Dull Knife's band with the Sioux? And there are many contradictions to be resolved, particularly about the events in Rawlins and Decatur counties. I have township maps of these counties on my walls and am working out the material with the places before my eyes.

Needless to say, I should like a look at any material pertaining to the Cheyennes. Is there any way I can see a copy of your old settler account from Rawlins county? I should not want you to trust an only copy to the mails. That holds true for any other material you may have. From middle August to December next fall I plan to make a last round of the Oklahoma-to-Wyoming regions. I aim to cover the entire Cheyenne region.

One incident of Cheyenne history—the destruction of a Cheyenne camp, men, women and children slaughtered on the Middle Fork of the Sappa, T5, R33, Rawlins County, April 23, 1875—needs clearing up. Most of the accounts I have are from the military and the buffalo hunters who took part. The Indians have been reluctant to speak of this, even to old friends like Grinnell. George Bent, half Cheyenne, hasn't been very explicit either. Perhaps, with all my material together, I can get the few old Cheyennes still alive to talk. "It is better forgotten" they sometimes tell me. But that was before I wrote *Crazy Horse*. Perhaps they will understand that I mean to defame no one. Thank you again for writing me, and assuming your approval, I am sending Senator Carmody a carbon of this letter.

Sincerely,

———

Eleanor Hinman

Dear Eli:

I don't hear how you are coming with your book. Did you receive the notes I sent you?

Now I have a query: In your "Oglala Sources," you have a note, page 33, saying that the Spider who was permitted with the injured Crazy Horse was American Horse; that Spider was a nick-name for American Horse. Do you recall anything more about this? Usually, Spider, among the Oglalas means the brother of Red Cloud. According to Document Files, 3–11–77, Department of the Platte, AGO Records, National Archives, Spider surrendered at Spotted Tail agency March 7, 1877. He is described as the brother of Red Cloud and "head of family" with many others in from the north. It's interesting that he surrendered at Spot's. Then 8–8-77, he is listed as on the way from Red Cloud for a scout with Hart into the north country, to return August 29.

As a northern Indian, even the brother of Red Cloud could have been permitted around the injured Crazy Horse, but I doubt whether the self-made Loafer chief, American Horse could have managed it so easily. The Cheyenne American Horse might have been there, however and might have been called Spider, although he is listed as gone south with Dull Knife and Little Wolf with Lawton in May, 1877.

This touches upon the real confusion in the blood relationships between the Oglalas and the Cheyennes. I've discovered that the Dull Knife family was closely related to Red Cloud, which may account for their decision to risk slipping in there, even with the country obviously so full of soldiers. The Dog Soldier band, not the society, was made up of mostly Cheyenne-Sioux, and Big Head, the Tangle Hair of the 1878 Cheyenne raid, was Sioux. Red Cloud's uncle, Red Cloud (father's brother) married into the Cheyennes and died a Cheyenne. The Loafer, American Horse, Three Bears, etc. were also closely related to the Northern Cheyennes, in addition to the

Cheyenne bloods among the Sioux, such as Little Big Man, etc. It becomes more and more difficult to think of the Cheyennes as a separate people, even the Southern branch, and yet there was a growing psychological differentiation—the result of a minority position in the time of pressures, from 1856 on, which makes a clearing up of the blood allegiances even more important.

I am anxious to clear up as much of this as I can before I return to the Tongue River and the southern agencies this fall. [. . .]

Sincerely,

———

JUNE 22, 1949

William Wade Head, Superintendent
Western Oklahoma Consolidated Agency
Anadarko, Oklahoma

I am finishing up the research for my book on the Cheyennes, a companion volume to my Sioux biography, *Crazy Horse,* published in 1942. I began the actual work on the Cheyenne book back in 1930 although I had a vast amount of material from my childhood around the Cheyennes who were friends of my father's and came to see him—Cheyennes who were on Pine Ridge when he came west in the [1880s] or were intermarried with the Oglalas and Brules.

Since 1930 I've put much time into this book. I spent two winters in Washington going through the AGO Records and the Records of the Indian Bureau for the Sioux and Cheyenne books, and I made several trips up into the Tongue river country since that first one in 1930, because the Northern Cheyennes and their region were so closely connected with the Crazy Horse story.

However, now I am done with all the records, manuscripts, and printed material available outside of the Montana and Oklahoma that I have been able to uncover and so I am coming out there to finish up sometime this fall, early in September, I hope. I should like to talk to such old timers as there are left, to get their point of view, and to clear up some confusions in names and in family relationships that have appeared as I wrote my preliminary draft.

I am mailing you a copy of my *Crazy Horse* for your personal library. If you have time to glance into it, and feel that my work is not too bad, will you send me the names of some of the old timers who might be willing to talk to me? There will be no pay involved in this. I never expect to get my investment of money out of this book any more than I did out of *Crazy Horse*, let alone anything for the five years of solid work which such books require. But I am happy to do this as long as I can keep myself financed in my modest way, to other more popular writing.

I wish I could come to the west earlier, but I can't until after the close of the Writer's Institute at Wisconsin, where I have charge of the advanced fiction writing courses. I regret this, but it is necessary.

While I'll be working in the period prior to 1880 in the book, if there is anything on which the Cheyennes might like a little publicity, say their arts and crafts, their cattle, and so on, I have some editorial friends who might be interested in an article on the contemporary scene. However, the book is the most important thing that I could be doing. There are so few of us left who knew any of the old buffalo hunters and have any writing ability.

Sincerely,

––––––––

AUGUST 7, 1949

Mr. Rufus Wallowing, Chairman
Council of Northern Cheyenne
Tongue River Agency
Lame Deer, Montana

Dear Mr. Wallowing:

Superintendent John Hunter kindly sent me your name as Chairman of the Council, and the man who can give me the names of some of the old Cheyennes who might be willing to assist me in getting as clear a picture as possible of the major events of the period from 1857 to 1880. I enclose a copy of the letter to Mr. Hunter.

You will see that I am particularly anxious to clear up some points on which the Cheyennes have been understandably reluctant to speak freely in the past. For example, there are such appalling attacks on them as the one on the Sappa creek, April 1875, by Lieutenant Henely and the buffalo hunters. Most of the accounts of this are from the white man's point of view. Grinnell makes only short mention of this fight, and Wooden Leg, in his story, *The Man who Fought with Custer* gives only a side glimpse or two at this. Yet, according to my notes, these were the Cheyennes who fled from the attack in the sandhills of Oklahoma, where the Indians retreated over the fighting when their men were being ironed for the trip to the prison at

Ft. Marion, Florida, and that the survivors carried the Sacred Arrows to the north, and that some were in the Custer fight. If this is true, then the men in that Sappa camp in 1875 were important men, and important or not, such a brutal attack on the camp, with women and children there, should be told. According to my notes the Indians offered a flag of truce and were denied surrender but were shot down. Whatever the truth is, I want it.

There are many other things I wish to know about, and many confusions in names and relationships to clear up. I hope that you and your people will find it in your hearts to help when I come up in early September. The Cheyenne story is the story of a noble people; I hope to measure up to its greatness as nearly as I can.

Sincerely,

———

OCTOBER 25, 1949

Edward Weeks

Dear Ted:

Back in exile, and taking it with poor grace. It was wearing, this living in a suitcase for four months, but people, friends and strangers alike, made me feel like a beloved homecomer everywhere, from Billings all the way down to the Washita. I walked over every great Cheyenne battlefield except one, the Sandhill fight on the North Fork of the Canadian, and that has been completely washed away in the seventy five years since then, and almost washed from the memory of men too, except that I scared up one old timer who remembered where it was, and how it looked before the water swept it away.

At home the family had a porcupine dinner for me. Our porky tribe lives entirely on corn and so has no taste of bark or pine, but turns out like a cross between goose and pork, only sweeter.

Jules and Flora took me around to look at all the little lost valleys until I found the one that fit exactly the description of the central point where Little Wolf hid his people from the U. S. Army, cavalry and infantry [during] the winter of 1878-9. They had one little hidden valley to which they withdrew whenever the scouts reported more soldiers and scouts out. It is perfectly hidden, the little valley is, that even with wood and water and grass enough for the pony herds it can't be detected unless one knows exactly where to look. Next day Boris, Flora's husband, took me over that way in the Cub and couldn't believe that such a valley could lie so close to his usual course for the northern airports and he never [saw] it. Even from

1200 foot elevation it was difficult to see unless we were exactly over it. Only an Indian who knew every foot of the country would have known where to go.

It was there, in Little Chokecherry, that an escaped warrior brought word to Little Wolf that all their relations with Dull Knife had been wounded or killed up beyond Fort Robinson.

Then Caroline took me up to the Northwest corner of Nebraska. We looked over the ground where Yellow Hand, the Cheyenne, was killed. By Buffalo Bill, Ned Buntline's publicity said, but 100 eyewitnesses always denied that. From Fort Robinson we followed the path of Dull Knife's flight over the bluffs where the half-clothed, starving men, women and children fled for 13 days in sub-zero weather. It was fitting that the gully where the final massacre ended the break was in a great bluff-walled saucer, with badland buttes rising here and there from the bottom—steep and gray and grooved as old ash piles. - - - Even today this terrain has a strange, remote, and forgotten look. Nobody around the region seems to know where the final battleground was, and it is perfectly credible, the story that the Indians tell, that eight of their people vanished in that flight and were never heard from again, their bones not found. One would not expect anyone to return from there.

I am sorry to ramble on so, but it's important to get these impressions down in rough shape, so you suffer.

Sincerely,

———

AUGUST 1, 1950

Dear Lee Casey:

Arthur Vetter of Denver sends me the clippings of your column and Robert Perkin's interview with Richard Bergen on the second Battle of Sitting Bull in the *Rocky Mountain News*.

Of course Sitting Bull was an Oglala Sioux chief, that is, the one called Sitting Bull the Good, the Oglala who was also known as Drum Packer. He was the nephew of Little Wound, chief of the Cut-Off Oglalas, and was often called son by him, in the Indian manner. This man, a great warrior in his early days, became a great friendly later and saved the lives of many whites at various times, notably in the Flag Pole troubles of 1874 at Red Cloud Agency, Nebraska. In May 1875 he and Red Cloud headed the Oglala Sioux delegation to Washington. There he was presented with a brass (gold washed) mounted rifle engraved to Sitting Bull in gratitude and friendship from the President of the United States. In the late fall of 1876, this Sitting Bull the Good was killed by General Miles' Crow scouts at Cantonment, Fort Keogh, near Miles City, Montana, while bringing in representatives of the hostiles under a white flag to parley with the General for the surrender of Crazy Horse and the other southern Sioux and their Cheyenne allies.

See my *Crazy Horse*. His gift rifle, picked up where he had left it lying behind in peace, reached the hands of General Miles and much later landed in the museum of the American Indian, Heye Foundation, New York, with the Miles collection. Naturally, without specific information to the contrary, it was labeled the rifle of Sitting Bull the Hunkpapa Medicine Man, since it came from up in the Hunkpapa region. I am told that the labeling was promptly changed when I presented the evidence that the gun belonged to Sitting Bull the Good, the Oglala.

Understanding that the Indians too have duplications in names was too much for the writers of the times, and the two men became one even in the eyes of many later historians, although the Indian bureau and the army officers of the agencies were never confused about them. Their reports clearly called the one "The Good" and the other the "Hunkpapa."

For years I had been trying to answer all the queries that came to me about the apparent treachery of Sitting Bull, the Hunkpapa, who seemed to have gone to Washington in friendship in 1875 and accepted the gift rifle and then, little more than a year later, was at the least a powerful defender against Custer's attack on the camps along the Little Big Horn.

But one cannot make a flat statement: Sitting Bull was two men without proof, so I was always having to copy out three pages of source material. Finally I put the information into an article published in Blue Book, November 1949. Now usually a card with that reference is enough for the queries that come in, sometimes from as far away as Switzerland, where Sitting Bull is a great psychological mystery, apparently.

Sincerely,

———

DECEMBER 14, 1950

Dr. EP Wilson
Chadron, NE

Dear Dr. Wilson:

Thank you for your fine long letter about my [Indian] pictures. I had tried most of the sources you suggest, but I was glad to have them reviewed in my mind. I went through all the Colorado Society pictures when I lived in Denver, the identified and the others, as well as those at the Denver library (where the Barry collection landed) and those at the Chappell House, where Denver city collection of American Indian material is housed, or was, and that is also a good one. I know Kubista slightly; he was a good friend of my father's. His work was good, but too new, and so far as I have been able to determine, he has little that is old except a few stock figures.

About Lame Deer—I am almost a resident up there. I was there again in 1949 for five weeks. They use the pathetic picture of the Custer captives taken on the Sweetwater in 1869 for Dull Knife, which was, of course, false, Custer never laid a hand on the Northern Cheyennes.

I contacted the McGregors some years ago for the society about the Cheyennes too, because they were at Lame Deer for a while. Like most other people, they never got the Little Wolfs quite clear in their minds. They were there too late and the one I want, the leader in the outbreak with Dull Knife had already been forgotten to the tongue of the Cheyennes, as they put it, because he had been the victim of such tragedy—as you know, he killed Starving Elk while drunk at Keogh, 1879–80, and became the humblest of his people after that, not even riding a horse. He never sat in a council after that, or smoked the long pipe. His nephew, Young Chief Little Wolf, became the leader of the Little Wolf people and with the complication of the several others of the name at the time, it's really confusing. [. . .]

Yes, He Dog lived with his Eagle Hawk relatives at Oglala, S. D. when I knew him. These people used to come down to the Niobrara in my child-hood and when I went to see He Dog in 1930–31, he was living with them. We also went to the Young Man Afraid family, but they knew nothing of the Crazy Horse material first hand anymore. As you say, they are a great Oglala family.

Incidentally, do you know what became of the Little Wound papers? These covered the Red Cloud agency period, sod and on the White River, the winter of Yellow Medicine and the return, and the establishment of the present Pine Ridge, with the Red Cloud-McGillycuddy troubles, etc. The Oklahoma University Press has another manuscript of Hyde's, covering the Oglalas through the agency period, but in reading it, I missed much information that I know is in the Little Wound collection. I hope it has not been lost.

[. . .]

A good 1951 to you,

———

Mr. A.M. Jones
Dover, Minn.

Dear Mr. Jones:

Thank you for your long letter about my *Reader's Digest* article and Jack Red Cloud. Red Cloud is a very common name among Indians. I know of at least a dozen among the Teton Sioux in the 1850–1890 period, and then there are many among the Minnesota Sioux. There was no contact of the extent your story would require between the Oglalas and the Minnesota Wisconsin region in the 1850–90 period, nor was Jack Red Cloud away from Pine Ridge agency in 1880. His name appears on every issue roster.

I don't recall Jack Red Cloud personally, of course. He was in the Crook fight of 1876, married Her Roan Horse and lived on his father's agency continuously throughout his lifetime. I've seen many pictures of him and he seems not only Indian, but full blood. I knew Jack's son, Jim Red Cloud, born 1879 over a period of many years and he couldn't have been half white.

Not that any of this prevents your story from being true, but it was most probably another Red Cloud. This story of the stolen white boy or girl, to appear as a grown Indian later is a very common one from the eastern seaboard to Puget Sound. There are just enough actual cases of white assimilation into the tribes, such as Cynthia Ann Parker, and the white woman who spent her life among the Arapahos, etc. to make one cautious about dismissing any account that comes up.

About the Fireclouds: some of those perhaps have white blood, and even if it were not true, Indians differ so in features that one can find a resemblance to almost anyone. Newspapermen claimed that Dull Knife was a dead ringer for Seward and in some not-to-well authenticated pictures, there does seem to be some resemblance.

Sincerely,

———

PS. Jack Red Cloud apparently never spoke much English.

Marvin F. Kivett, Director,
Museum, Nebraska State Historical Society
State Capitol, Lincoln 9, Nebraska

Dear Mr. Kivett:

I am happy to hear the new building is coming along so well. Yes, I thought about the building too, when the clippings of Mr. Hill's death came in. They brought back so many things of my days around the Society, so much of A.T.'s determination, his single-mindedness, his lusty humor and his warm heartedness.

About the "buckskin shirt" made by Black Dog for Rainwater: As I recall, much of the Zimmerman Collection was Brule Sioux. Certainly this shirt seems to be Brule. Black Dog was head of a camp of the peaceful, the Laramie Sioux allied with Big Mouth. I find him in this association in 1867 in Bratt, page 115, etc. As you know, Big Mouth was originally a Bad Face Oglala and was encouraged to leave them by various factors. He joined the Loafers around Laramie and was associated with the Brules until he was killed. Whether Black Dog was also Oglala gone Brule I can't discover from my meager Sioux index here. He was a shirt maker for various Brules. Either he or one of his relatives made some of the ghost dance shirts, for there is a ghost dance pattern among the Brules called the Black Dog pattern. I don't have the distinguishing markings of this shirt in my mind and my index on this is still in storage. You might be able to check it through Mooney, etc.

The Brules had a chieftain society similar to but not quite the same as the Shirtwearers of the Oglalas. Unfortunately much less has been done on the specific organizations of the Brules than the Oglalas.

I find a couple of references to Rainwater in my index here, both apparently Brules, but whether they are two men or one, I can't say. Perhaps a check of the Brule signers to the treaty of 1889 [?] could give you a line on both Rainwater and Black Dog. [. . .] As I recall, Rainwater was a younger man than Black Dog, who seemed somewhere near the age of Big Mouth, from my references.

Perhaps there is some reference to these men in Standing Bear's books or the Bettelyoun manuscript.

Sincerely,

———

Mr. Donald E. Stewart
Encyclopedia Britannica
425 N. Michigan Ave.

Chicago, Illinois

Dear Mr. Stewart:

In your letter of May 27, replying to my query why there is no reference to peyote in the *Britannica*, you say "the drink mescal which is obtained from the leaves of the maguey" is mentioned in the article "Agave." That has very little pertinency to the subject. The top of the peyote cactus happens to be called mescal button, but the plant is not related to the mescal from which the drink is made.

Peyote is important because it produces a kind of hypnotic trance with hallucinations and has been the center of controversy for around a hundred years, ever since its use began to spread out of our southwest. It was a problem for the missionaries of the southwest and later on the western Indian reservations also, and for the physicians and law enforcement officers, with much marshalling of evidence for and against the drug. Peyote was involved in the Ghost Dance troubles of the late 1880s and early 1890s, and it was said by some to have been the basis of Empress Carlotta's mental breakdown. There is still controversy over its possible habit-forming power. But whether it is habit-forming or not, its proponents consider it the secret behind the quieter, more contented factions on the Indian reservations, as far east as Wisconsin and the Great Lakes regions by now. I hear there is some use of peyote among the Spanish peoples of New York.

Peyote is the basis of the Native American Church to which an increasing number of our Indians are turning, although the drug has been preached against and outlawed. At present many who are interested in the American Indian, in and out of the government service, tend to approve the use of peyote as a legitimate part of the ritual of the church, something like the sacramental wine. But there are many who consider peyote the greatest single force for Indian degradation. There are peyote songs published and recorded everywhere. I bought records of some of these songs here on East 42nd street and I recorded some around the Sioux of Pine Ridge, South Dakota. I've heard them sung in Oklahoma, Montana and Minnesota.

Because it is known that I work in the Indian field, I receive many queries about peyote, mostly from people who have gone through the usual elementary research sources, including the *Britannica*, and found nothing. With the long and growing interest in this subject I find your omission annoying, perhaps because it demands so much of my time to make up your lack of information. I also find the omission baffling, and your reply to my letter about peyote even more so. There are hundreds of doctors who could write you a few cogent lines on this subject.

Yours truly,

———

NOVEMBER 11, 1953

F.H. Sinclair

Dear Neckyoke:

[. . .] I am very sorry about this delay in acknowledging your long letter.

The work you and your wife are doing for the young Indians touches me very deeply. There's so little done for them in a constructive way—to help them develop into self-reliance, into self confidence and responsibility. I trust your Indian Day went well. Several of my acquaintances went out and sent back post cards, but I've been too busy to visit with them and get the news.

Yes, I know of Julia Wild Hog. She was in the Outbreak. They wintered in Lost Chokecherry Valley, near the head of Snake River, a tributary to the Niobrara in northwestern Nebraska. [. . .] I ran into Julia in 1931, either at Kate Bighead's or some of the other Indians' homes. I recall that she was uncommunicative then. Fortunately, I didn't wonder at their attitude; it was a very tragic time, that year, and the things that led up to it. I wonder if my story [*Cheyenne Autumn*] might not help you get her story from her. I used to know one of her relatives, perhaps her great-aunt, very well. She was the aunt of Little Finger Nail, one of the warriors killed in the last hole up in the Hat Creek bluffs about Robinson, with the Dull Knife people.

Yes, according to my files, George Bent belonged to the Chiefs Society of the Southern Cheyennes. You are really honored to be inducted by the Northerners. They generally shy away from whites much more than the Southerners ever did, even from white blood it seems to me. And it's not surprising.

I agree with you on the Crazy Horse statue being carved at the Black Hills. My European correspondents complain that Ziolkowski's conception is too Germanic, with the heavy-muscled, round chest figure, with the hair blowing back. But, I am still in favor of the statue, for we'll probably never get a good one if it is left too long, but if there is a commemorating figure, someone may come along later and get more Indian feeling into it. In the meantime we have something for Americans to think about.

[. . .]

Sincerely, and in haste,

———

DECEMBER 17, 1953

Mr. Thomas M. Galey
Box 544, Owensboro, Kentucky

Dear Mr. Galey:

Yes, Black Horse, the Cheyenne, was in the flight north in 1878. He was also in the 1875 flight, the time he got his leg injury while he was being ironed for prison in Florida. The story of this is told in my *Cheyenne Autumn*, in a very compressed form. There is a filed account, from the trooper's side, in the National Archives (War Records), in Washington, D.C. and more from the buffalo hunter's side in Wheeler, and in various manuscripts scattered over the west. This 1875 outbreak is barely mentioned by Grinnell, mainly because the Indians wouldn't talk about it. Not until I could say, "This is the way the white man tells it. If this is not the truth, you can see that I must tell your side, or I will have to use the story I have," would they tell me anything about 1875.

Your photograph of Black Horse and Bull Hump, the son of Dull Knife, taken in 1920 are fine items. We owe a debt to every photographer of the old buffalo hunters. I only wish we had done better about preserving the photographs that were taken. So many that I saw constantly in my childhood have disappeared completely, or so it seems.

The Bull Hump of the Black Kettle campaign was another man, an older one. The name is common and with considerable honor among the Cheyennes, as is the name Little Wolf. I had a long, long and not too successful search finding good pictures of Dull Knife and Little Wolf, both dead long before you were on the reservation, of course. In my childhood, there were many [photographs] of both men around in northwest Nebraska. Old Cheyenne Woman, who was at our place many days in my childhood, usually when some of her friends came to pick potatoes up on the Mirage Flats, had pictures of both men made at Fort Robinson the spring of 1877, but these are all gone, so far as I know. Oh, there are plenty labeled as of these two men, but they usually prove to be of someone else. The labeling at the Bureau of Ethnology is shockingly inaccurate, due to errors before they were catalogued there. There was once a tendency to change labels on pictures to suit whatever Indian was in the news at the moment.

[. . .]

Thank you for your fine letter and your exceptional interest in the American Indian. I hope you are putting your material into some shape for the public.

Best wishes for a good 1954,

———

FEBRUARY 16, 1954

Mr. Douglas T. Barker,
832 Bachellor Ave.,
Linden, N.J.

Dear Mr. Barker:

I am sorry my *Cheyenne Autumn* disturbed you. I moderated much contained in the *Proceedings of the Board of Officers* that investigated the Dull Knife outbreak at Fort Robinson. The details of the atrocities committed against the Cheyennes recorded there are almost impossible for even a hardened old historian like myself to read.

Apparently I did not make one of my points sufficiently clear. I did not intend this book as an indictment of the white man only. I am convinced that any minority that possesses something the majority wants is in danger of dispossession, even extermination. Sooner or later, some individual or group willing to go to any length to expropriate the minority will rise to power. Knowing this, there have long been those who worked for some international body to whom minorities could appeal, long, long, before the League of Nations or the U.N.

If you are interested in the American Indians there is still work to be done for them. Just now they are being turned over to the states without the consent of the Indians. Their oil, coal, and uranium holdings, no longer supervised by the federal trusteeship, which demanded contracts comparable to those that the white man could get, will soon be stolen from them. True, the federal government in many cases has been very lax in providing the adequate education promised in our treaties, so the Indians often cannot read even a newspaper, let alone a contract. This situation was known to both political parties. Hoover put out a lovely and lengthy volume that denounced the reservation schools and the lack of training for self-sufficiencies in his administration but then did nothing to remedy the situation created by a long line of predecessors and perpetuated by his own administration.

Sincerely,

———

FEBRUARY 22, 1954

James W. Waters
1212 Elberts Circle,
Covington, Ky.

Dear Mr. Waters:

The Sioux always claimed that the white man never understood their systems of chieftanships, perhaps because it varied some between the different divisions, say the Oglalas and Hunkpapas, for instance. I think it's accepted that we know more about the Oglala scheme than the others partly through Clark Wissler's "Societies and Ceremonial Associations in the Oglala Division of the Teton-Dakotas" Anthropological Papers, The American Museum of Natural History, Vol. II, pt. 1; through the work of Helen Blish, mentioned in my *Crazy Horse*; Neihardt's *Black Elk Speaks*, and in the workings of the chieftainships in my book, as it was worked out with old He Dog, Red Feather, and others who knew the old pre-reservation system. Since the Hunkpapa chieftain society was different from the Oglala Shirtwearer's society, comparison is difficult. Many say that Sitting Bull was never a chief in the sense that Crazy Horse was, as a Shirtwearer, but this is very probably a misunderstanding of the Hunkpapa system. The fact that the Bull was a great medicine dreamer is not against his being a forceful and powerful chief. At least he had the following, as a political leader, and that makes a chief in fact if not in title. He was not a chief of the white man's selection for the agency, men in most cases (with the exception of Spotted Tail), held in some contempt by the Indians because their elevation was based upon the workings of white men rather than the Indians.

When you get into the Cheyennes, there the system is clear and tight and unchanging during the period of close white man contact prior to the agency days. Dull Knife was one of the four Old Man Chiefs of the Northern Division, as Black Kettle was in the Southerners. Yellow Hand didn't live to be more than one of the nine little chiefs of his soldier band. Roman Nose refused elevation into even the forty band chiefs, as I say in *Cheyenne Autumn*. Quanah Parker was a Comanche chief but their system varied greatly from the rather similar ones of the Sioux and Cheyennes, in the larger sense at least. For some reason, the system under which Washakie was made chief is not clear. As the Shoshonis were friendly with the whites from Washakie's boyhood, there is no telling now how much of his prominence was aided by the white man's favors and presents. This was not true for the Comanches' chieftainships; they were hostiles (most of the time) and their chiefs were their own in Parker's day.

Chief Joseph's long friendship with the whites may have had the aid from the whites, although he certainly measured up as a great leader when the test came. Experts in the Nez Perce tell me that much of the genius of the retreat of that tribe was due to other men, notably Looking Glass. But I've done no research among these Indians and Indian sources so I only know what white men have written. And, that's generally not sufficiently grounded in actual Indian sources to be very revealing in these more intimate matters. Cochise is entirely out of my territory.

One can't expect to be expert in diverse Indians of diverse cultural and geographic environment[s]. You are interested in these various Indian leaders, why don't you write such a compendium or Index book as you mention? None of us who have worked to become expert in a tribe or two could do this because no one life time is long enough to become an expert in all the tribes you bring up and, we would not be content to accept less of ourselves. [. . .]

Anyway, I wish you success with your undertakings,

———

JUNE 5, 1954

Mr. E.S. Sutton
Hazelhurst Farms
Benkelman, Nebraska

Dear Mr. Sutton:
There's no livelier topic in western history that the purported photographs of Crazy Horse, the Oglala war chief and one time Shirtwearer. One confusion is the number of men actually named so—meaning Mystical or Holy, Inspired Horse. The ease of confusion becomes evident when

one looks at the list of signers of the 1889 Sioux treaties about changes in reservation lands. There was, as I recall now, four Sioux named Crazy Horse of sufficient prominence to sign that treaty, three from Pine Ridge. One of these was formerly named Greasy Head but after Crazy Horse's death in 1877, he married his widow, the Larabee woman and, by good Sioux custom, took his illustrious predecessor's name. Men like He Dog always referred to this one as Crazy Horse II. This is the dark little man with war bonnet (an adornment the Oglala war chief never wore) and sometimes a drum who appears on postcards labeled Crazy Horse. Then there is the northern breed who was often photographed on the far upper Missouri with a Hudson Bay blanket coat, etc. and a southern Indian down around Ft. Yuma or thereabouts, who was photographed in 1874 and widely circulated.

Now to the "Crazy Horse" in the *World-Herald*, May 16, 1954: This is a face-on picture of Standing Bear, the Ponca chief, with horns added to his feather headdress as he did for certain ceremonial occasions. If you will look on page 227, Vol. II Morton and Watkin's *History of Nebraska*, there are exactly the same two people in a larger, clearer picture, the Indian dressed in exactly the same accoutrements, with the same decorative designs, in side view, labeled "Julius Meyer and Standing Bear."

Julius Meyer was in close contact with the Poncas and Omahas. He was in Washington with the May 1875 Indian delegations, including Oglalas and Brule Sioux, and had his picture taken with the agency Oglala and Brule chiefs. See page 234 of the *History of Nebraska* above. (The Sitting Bull here is, of course, the Good, the Minor, the Oglala. On this trip he was presented the "gold" mounted rifle by President Grant which I describe in my article "The Two Sitting Bulls" in *Blue Book Magazine*, November 1949.) Meyer had no such close contact with Crazy Horse, who was never in Washington or Omaha, etc.

[...]
Sincerely,

———

JUNE 9, 1954

Emmie Mygatt

Dear Emmie Mygatt:
It's fine to hear from you, and about the Cheyennes, and although I am busy, and preparing for surgery next week, I must write you what I know

I Do Not Apologize

of the lance you picture. This is certainly one of the two crooked lances that belonged to the Elk Society (Little Wolf's) sometimes called Elk-Horn Scrapers, or, as Grinnell spells it, the Himoweyuhkis. These were shaped into a shepherd's crook at one end. (The other two lances of the society were straight.) These four lances were carried by the bravest men of the society. The shafts were wrapped partially and one, I think wholly to the head, in strips of otter skin and at four different points along the shaft two eagle feathers were tied. The lances were carried on formal war parties which were led by the Elks, and in dances of the Elks and in the large dances in which various soldier societies took part. See Grinnell's *The Cheyenne Indians*. I think Mrs. Petter at the agency would have a copy and certainly someone at Sheridan if not the library.

The Elk Soldiers was one of the six military societies of the Cheyennes: others were Fox, Shield, Bowstring, Dog Soldiers, and Northern Crazy Dogs. Other names for the Elks were Hoof Rattle, Crooked Lance, Headed Lance, Medicine Lance, and Elk-Horn Scrapers.

At the time of the revenge against the Kiowas for the killing of the Bowstring men, 1838, Medicine Water, Little Old Man and White Antelope were the chiefs of the Elks along. Roman Nose and George Bent were both later men of this society; Big Crow, head chief of the society was prominent in the attack on Julesburg, 1/7/1865. The men carrying the crooked lances and the straight ones of this society led the advance on Platte Bridge the summer of 1865. Roman Nose, killed in the 1868 Beecher Island battle, made one of the medicine lances I've been told, after the original was destroyed in a fire.

The Elk soldiers had the best runners of the Northern Cheyennes including such men as Apache, Little Wolf and his son, Wooden Thigh and Wooden Leg. Left Hand Shooter and Feathered Wolf also belonged. Other prominent Elks were Old Bear and Little Shield, etc.

At the time of the Custer battle, Bobtail Horse, Lame White Man, Left Hand Shooter, Broken Jaw, Pig, Crow Cut Nose, Goes After Other Buffalo, Plenty Bears, White Hawk, Wolf Medicine and Tall White Man were in the fight.

Perhaps you can help save the old Crooked Lance with this great group of Northern Cheyennes.

Mari Sandoz

———

DECEMBER 4, 1954

Floyd J. Schmitz
430 Morris St.
Oglesby, Illinois

Dear Mr. Schmitz:

Thank you for the nice letter and kind words about *Crazy Horse*.

Warbonnet, using the term to cover all the fancy headgear of the Plains Indians, usage differed very much, both among the Sioux and the Cheyennes. Most of the fine ones, particularly those with the long tails, were part of the ceremonial regalia and not to be risked in battle. Some were ceremonial and for a formal war attack, the kind initiated by carrying the pipe around several bands of a tribe or even to various tribes, as in the march northward after the Sand Creek attack the fall of 1864, or in the concerted Cheyenne attack on the Kiowas to avenge the Bowstring soldiers. There was this kind of formality before the attack on Ft. Phil Kearny that ended in the Fetterman fight, etc.

Then there were the soldier chieftain bonnets of the society selected by the council to protect a village on the move or in camp. If attacked, a few of the so called little chiefs would put on their bonnets to signify their office and their position of honor and obligation at that time. For instance, the round bonnets of crow feathers were often seen in fights that involved the fleeing of a village. As the Dog Soldiers were sworn to protect the rear of any village, their little chiefs often wore the bonnets. But these are not the kind of thing you see in the artist's conception of a warbonnet. Another point to remember: much more of the old-time regalia for war showed up in fights against Indian enemies than against white soldiers.

The fight on the Little Big Horn was an unusual circumstance, an attack on a great summer ceremonial gathering of many bands of the Sioux and some guests from other tribes. This kind of attack never happened before on the Plains and much was left to the individual's choice. Truly ceremonial bonnets were not worn, I am told. War of any kind defiles them. Other types of bonnets were worn by a few, but a very few.

There were always some bonnets tied in with the [warriors'] battle medicine and some of these wore them. But such bonnets are not the fine long-tailed ones of great value. (As late as 1910 the Sioux paid my father $5 for the two downy feathers under the tail of the eagle for the true ceremonial bonnet). These long-tailed bonnets were usually the accoutrements of council chiefs, the Shirtwearers too, and none of these were to take part in active fighting except in actual village hand-to-hand battles, not any more than our senate or cabinet members would fight in the front lines. These ceremonial bonnets were often used as a badge of office and a head chief of a camp might clap his on his head if the place was surprised, to run out and show the white flag of surrender with authority. Medicine Arrow did this on the Sappa in 1875, to show that his surrender was official.

One thing that confuses the white man is the Indian artist's habit of painting the warriors in full regalia in war. This is their way of identifying the men. Anyone familiar with the tribal regalia can tell at least the man's position in his camp, his warrior society and often something of his family by the accoutrements given him in the picture. Those who knew the special medicine of the individuals can tell just who the man was, by name. They used this method instead of our use of captions. I took a lot of Indian pictures, Cheyenne and Sioux, to the Indians. Many turned out to be of the Reno and Custer fights, and in the interpretation the Indians could tell me just who the men were—the Cheyennes the Sioux warriors and vice versa, by the accoutrements. But when I asked how the men fought, I found that usually they had gone in stripped to the breech-clout and moccasins and paint, a few in leggings. Almost none except the surprised Hunkpapas had shirts on, and few of those, for the day was a hot one.

The trouble with your pursuit of an old Sioux warbonnet is that the fine old article has gone to pieces, at least unless protected from air, heat, and moisture. Feathers don't last long and even at the best, they fade and break.

[. . .]

Well, this is a hasty attempt to answer your questions.

Sincerely,

————

NOVEMBER 5, 1955

Mr. Henry Smith
927 Iowa Avenue
Colton, California

Dear Mr. Smith:

[. . .]

About Lincoln's attitude toward the American Indians: I got my information from the material in War Records, now in the National Archives, but stored over on Virginia Avenue when I went through the years 1850–1879 back in 1937–38, and in the records of the Indian Bureau, then in the Bureau storage files. There were endless protests and appeals to Lincoln over the extermination policy inaugurated by such men as General Harney in the 1850s, and carried on under Lincoln. The pressures that brought on the so-called Minnesota Massacres were sanctioned by Lincoln, although delegations of both whites and Indians tried to get to him. Those who managed to see him were told the story of his experiences as an enlistee in the Black Hawk war—the story of helping to bury the whites killed. So it was with Lincoln's full knowledge that the peaceful, Christianized Sioux of Minnesota were driven to rise up in the Minnesota Massacres, 1862, and the so-called leaders tried and executed. Look up the history of the Santee Sioux (who now live in Northeastern Nebraska) and the New Ulm Massacre, particularly the investigation of the whole Minnesota matter. My notes on these things are in storage but there's enough available in any good library to establish Lincoln's prejudicial attitude toward Indians.

[. . .]

No, it seems there is no good organization to help the Indian. Never given the schools and training the treaties promised, he is rapidly being entirely unlanded by this administration. The Sioux of South Dakota live in tents and Hooverville shacks in the Nebraska towns, now from Chadron to Omaha.

Sincerely,

————

NOVEMBER 3, 1956

Mr. William B. Secrest
4723 E. Brown
Fresno, California

Dear Mr. Secrest:

I'm happy that you enjoyed *The Buffalo Hunters* and particularly with your extensive interest in western history.

[. . .] One thing we must remember about such killings of Indians: from 1850 on, all the power of the propaganda media of the times was used to make the Sioux (the Noble Red Man until 1850, when we didn't want his region very intensely) a savage, a sub-human who could be exterminated without too much protest, in fact, should be exterminated. Very few buf-

I Do Not Apologize

falo hunters had any compunction about killing defenseless Indians, even women and infant children. And why should they when even under the great humanitarian Lincoln you could have the Sand Creek massacre, or earlier, the butchery of Little Thunder's band on the Blue Water, or Dull Knife's people at Fort Robinson later, in 1879, or the Sioux at Wounded Knee?

Properly conditioned, any people will produce a good percent of men (and women) who look upon the extermination of those who differ from them (and have something they want) as the proper destruction of a predatory animal. It's not only the Nazis that do these things, or the woolhat boys of the south. We can all be led down this path if the approach is insidious enough. It wasn't only Sheridan who preached extermination. That was government policy from 1855 on. And earlier, it was the policy in Colonial New England, and before that—clear back into pre-history.

I realize that most of us who have intellectual interests, and are sufficiently humanized to have some consideration for other peoples, are inclined to forget that man is often a [compartmentalized] creature, with whole areas in which his ethical code doesn't operate at all.

I'm sorry. This weak spot in the armor of one of the most admirable creatures, man, is a sorrow to me and I get carried away.

Sincerely,

———

JULY 7, 1957

Dear Father Powell:

[...]

I am happy to hear that the work of Senators Douglas and Murray promises enough so the Brules see some cause for optimism. In the fall of 1954, some Brules came down into the Sandhills for a few hours visit with me, and, although they were strangers and a little inarticulate, they were plainly deeply disturbed with the times and the rapid unlanding of the Indians. They hoped to salvage something of their past for generations to come and offered to help me any way they could if I would come to Rosebud to gather material for a book on Spotted Tail. Of course I couldn't, and it was sad all around.

[...]

About the Amos Bad Heart Bull manuscript: I'm pleased that you have the photostats. I think the last I knew of the picture history itself was that it was back with the Bad Heart Bull family up near Oglala, and let's hope there has been no fire. I've agitated occasionally for a full color reproduction of the entire book, not only for the beauty of it but for the meaning, which is often lost in black and white. A full color book, with the Blish interpretations for the Indians would be a fine piece of work for Carnegie, since they paid for Helen's work on it. They write me that there's no money, but there's always money for other things, I see. Perhaps I should start another round of agitation over at the Ford Foundation for something for Indian education and the preservation and publication of such Indian cultural material.

No, the He Dog whose camp is usually referred to on maps, the one over on the Rosebud, was not the brother-chieftain of Crazy Horse. That one was a Brule friendly, the one whose picture was taken in Washington in the early 1870s with a long eagle feather headdress. [The other] He Dog was over on the Pine Ridge Reservation back in the region the hostiles were given when they returned from Canada (where they fled after the killing of Crazy Horse). And while you're up around the Montana Indians, will you look around carefully for the inroads I hear peyote has made among them, particularly the Cheyennes? With its identification with the Native American Church, it's difficult to fight now, but I hear sad stories from up north. I can see how the frustrations and hopelessness of the Cheyennes' situation can drive one to such an escape but I still hope that the reports are exaggerated. I've seen some of the results of peyote among the Sioux too. It is the more imaginative and discerning ones who seem to be caught by it. However, it seems to keep the more protesting of the Indians quiet, so many approve of it. [. . .]

Good traveling—

———

APRIL 16, 1958

Henry Alsberg[11]
Hastings House

Dear Henry:
The whole business of scalping was overrated by the white men. It never got deeply rooted in the Plains Indians, and was only a symbol unless it was a scalp to be danced by some woman relative of the warrior. For that, they preferred Indian scalp locks, not white men tufts of hair. Particularly scalp locks of some traditional Indian enemy warriors. If there was a witness to the scalping, the scalp itself was no use even to a young warrior who

I Do Not Apologize

needed the count for a coup toward a position in the warrior society or toward eligibility as a husband of some important young woman. A tuft of horse hair would do just as well for the scalp dance, if there was one, and much better than a white man's scalp. Scalps were very often thrown away as soon as taken. Besides, this Plum Creek attack yielded bolts of calico, etc., that the warriors strung over the plains, to fly on the wind. Read the account in Grinnell. Here is a good glimpse of young Sioux having fun.

Good luck,

————

MARCH 27, 1959

Dear Bruce Nicoll:[12]

I've been thinking about the possible surviving relatives of Amos Bad Heart Bull and realize that of course there would be no old timer left, so there won't be any necessity for the old formal approach for your photographers in addition to the usual financial arrangement that would be made with any white owner of the picture history.

There were publishing arrangements signed with the Carnegie Foundation, but whether there was a time clause I do not recall.

The chief heir to Helen Blish's estate was an older sister, a Mrs. Doctor Joyner of Iowa. In New York I have this for about 1937–38, which is pretty old. The Iowa Medical association directory, or better, the AMA directory may cut down the time consumed in tracing the Joyners.

As I recall, the Carnegie people had the publication rights to both the pictures and the Blish narrative material but the time limit may have been reached.

Anyway, this is the most important single publishing venture, by volume, of the Great Plains. It is the fullest picture history in existence, as far as I know, with the greatest detail and artistry. Further, no other picture history has had anything like the intelligent and tireless interpretation by the old timers who took part in the events portrayed, events that include such fights and the Reno and Custer battles, etc. up to the battle at Wounded Knee, and intertribal fights. In addition there are many fine portrayals of ceremonials, with all the careful study and description by Helen Blish. All through this runs the philosophy and religion of the Oglala Lakota at his best.

I wish you every success—
In haste,

————

Dear Helen Schnidt:[13]

Yes, it is true that at both Haskell, in Kansas and Carlisle, Pa.,[14] the Indian children had to have their hair cut off. They did this in all the agency schools too. This was in keeping with the policy of breaking up all the external evidences of Indianness, to go along with the deliberate outlawing and destruction of the Indian's religion and his philosophical beliefs as well as his tribal organizations and ethical and social standards. As for the delousing—that was necessary in all the usual public schools of the 1870–80 period and much later. Even as late as my school days, both Jules[15] and I got head lice at school. The Polish kids had them and the thick braided daughters of George Peters too. Fine toothed combs were carried by all the stores and the wagon peddlers, for the one reason. Most of the Indian children were pretty clean headed around the reservations. The Indian women knew how to get rid of lice. [. . .]

If you are interested in Carlisle, see *Pratt, The Red Man's Moses* by Elaine Goodale Eastman (former teacher on Pine Ridge, and wife of Dr. Charles Eastman) the only book on the man responsible for the school. [. . .]

For a record of real brutalization in the Indian government schools see the report of the Hoover Commission. Their results were beautifully published, but of course Hoover did nothing about the situation—the general confinement, whipping, starvation, etc. Since the Indian Bill passed in August 1953, the bill that all the good newspapers begged Eisenhower not to sign, there has been steady degradation of the Indians. It's the old extermination policy in effect again, but without the honor of dying decently for your rights. Now they can only become sodden with peyote, liquor, and hopelessness on top of the generations of malnutrition.

The purpose has been during this administration to wrest the range, the coal, iron, oil, uranium, etc. from the Indian without giving him the same contracts or the same protection that a white man would have. There are 7 to 8 thousand Sioux in Chicago, I am told, many from the Dakota reservations, promised work there if they would sell out and go. But of course they were not prepared to handle the work, or the jobs they were promised were fictitious. The Indians need more land, enough to make a decent living, not less. Land, education, credit, and hope.

As for the old grandmothers hanging to the purse strings: Sioux were always a matrilineal society and the lodge, the home, and the family always belonged to the women.

I wonder why you try to fight the battles of the administration. You can't win. I know. Not within my adulthood was there an Indian administration that couldn't, if enough people tried, be improved some at least. Emmons wrote me that I was a New York City woman and I had no understanding of the western Indian problems when I wrote him.

Why fight the battles of the Indians' past injustices? Give your pupils the very best start you can, both in subject matter and in conduct—thoughtfulness and self-respect and you will have given them the greatest gift within your power. They have had so few teachers who saw them as human beings, as more than an inconvenient way of making a sort of living.

Look over your school tomorrow with all your love, and some of mine for them.

In haste,
Sincerely,

———

FEBRUARY 24, 1960

David H. Stroud
101 Brighton Ave.
Spring Lake, N.J.

Dear David Stroud:

Thank you, I'm always happy over a kind word about my *Crazy Horse*. It comes nearest to doing what I planned of any of my books.

About your Indian Collection: It sounds fine, particularly if you have evidence to prove your classification of the various items. [. . .]

About the collection's monetary value: I would be the last one to know that. I never think in such terms, or about private ownership of relics of any people except by the people themselves. I never accept anything from the Indians, nothing they try to give me that has any connection with their culture or the old days. These things I feel I have no claim to. They should remain with the families or be where everyone can see them, in good museums. Of course, I don't expect other people to feel as I do. I am deeply involved in these things.

I place a very high value upon authenticated items that reveal something of the life, historical, social, artistic and mystical of the old pre-reservation Indian, but I know that in our society the yardstick is always the commercial one—what's the going price? This usually has absolutely no relation to the intrinsic value of any item or collection. It's too bad. [. . .]

It's nice to hear from you and I regret that I can't give you any idea of the value of your collection.

Sincerely,

———

DECEMBER 18, 1960

Alvin M. Josephy[16]
American Heritage
551 Fifth Ave.
New York, 17, N.Y.

Dear Alvin:

Enclosed is a copy of terse notes from an item about Crazy Horse. I suppose that at the Museum of Natural History they showed you their copy of the Helen Blish manuscript on Amos Bad Heart Bull's picture history of the Hunkpatila band of Oglalas. There are two of these manuscripts, one a study of the art, the other the historical events portrayed in the picture history as interpreted by He Dog; Short Bull (both uncles of Amos Bad Heart Bull) and other hostiles out with Crazy Horse.

The trouble has always been that Crazy Horse never came near the trading posts or the agencies (except the time to run horses through the Fort Laramie parade ground) from the time he became a young warrior until the spring of 1877. Nobody knew anything specific about him.

There is, we are all convinced, no photograph of *this* Crazy Horse, although there are a half a dozen others with the same name, including the one usually sold—the picture of Greasy Head, who took the name of his illustrious predecessor when he married the breed widow of Crazy Horse. There were three or four Oglala and Brule signers of the name to the treaty of 1889. There was also a Hunkpapa of the name in 1875.

Good luck,

———

JUNE 5, 1961

Richard B. Williams,[17]
Sturgis Public Schools,
Sturgis, South Dakota.

Dear Richard Williams:

[. . .]

Congratulations on getting Bear Butte set aside as a State Park! I know something of the obstacles to such a bill and I am happy to know that my Sioux and Cheyenne books may have helped a little.

It is easy to establish something of the importance the Butte carried in the religious life of both of these tribes, but I hope that you will be able to delve farther back into the past. There must be prehistoric sites in the region, sites that you have perhaps already located.

I haven't been to Bear Butte for some years, but I recall standing alone on a sort of broken bank around the lower part and looking off east and southeast trying to imagine how it looked before the white man came, with perhaps water in this apparently dry run or that one. Off some distance from the sacred Butte there might have been corn patches, and on a second bench, the earth houses, perhaps set west of the water, to avoid mosquitoes in the prevailing westerly evening winds of the Plains.

If I was right, there should be plenty of sign around, if not rifled long ago. I suspect that there were temporary fire spots up closer than any dwellings, left by the temporary camps for the ceremonials. These might be in the path of the early sun's rays.

I'm making myself homesick with this letter. I wish that transportation weren't so impossible up to the Black Hills. [. . .] If it were easier to get around I'd run up and take a look at Bear Butte.

Sincerely,

———

APRIL 16, 1962

Mr. J. L. Smith
1915 40th St. Pl.
Des Moines, Iowa

Dear Mr. Smith:

You have been digging into the Sioux. It's a fertile field, never worn out.

I'll try to answer some of your queries: (most of my Sioux material unrelated to the Cheyennes is in storage out west.)

1. Evidently Crazy Horse, by his puberty dreaming and his medicine, belonged to no warrior or social societies. He was a member of the Chiefs

society, the Shirtwearers, which was an honor and accepted by making the Shirtwearer's vow, and lost by Crazy Horse through the incident with Black Buffalo Woman.

2. Crazy Horse was not a heyoka, a member of the Contraries, the Thunder Dreamers. He was a temporary Thunder cultist over a snow-thunder dream he invoked for a vision to guide him in the final saving of his people. See the Helen Blish manuscripts, copy with her sister, Mrs. Dr. Joyner, formerly of Iowa, now in Washington, D.C. Another copy is in the American Museum of Natural History.

3. The sacred Oglala lances come out of a dim time of prehistory, back around the headwaters of the Great Lakes. He Dog and Crazy Horse were the last to carry them, twice, it seems, from He Dog's account. (This material in storage.)

4. Crazy Horse had an elder sister, married to Club Man, older brother of the Little Killer who was an admiring follower of Crazy Horse. The sister had various names.

5. Yes, Crazy Horse had an older half brother (different mothers). He was called Horse Stands in Sight, and was killed in the North Platte valley. For a while the name was given to the brother, Crazy Horse, as was customary, since the name of one dead could not be spoken unless in the living.

6. I don't think Crazy Horse's medicine would have permitted the Hunka ceremony. Hump was in a curious mentor-father-brother-friend relationship with Crazy Horse, one that evolved gradually, I think.

Have you seen the Wissler and Walker *Anthropological Papers,* described on the enclosed slip?

Sincerely,

———

APRIL 16, 1962

Father Peter J. Powell
St. Timothy's Church
3555 West Huron Street
Chicago 24, Illinois

Dear Father Powell:
About your questions in the letter of April 8:

I Do Not Apologize

1. May the discrepancy in accounts of the Sacred Buffalo Hat of the Northern Cheyennes in war be a matter of interpretation of the prepositions
"to" and "into"? My understanding is that sometimes in a tribal attack,
the Hat was brought out and "worn" or carried in the formal move to
the battle site, and there was shown on a rise among the headmen who
directed the fight, as was sometimes true, apparently in a strong attack on
the village containing the Sacred Tipi of the Hat. Then it seems the Hat
was sometimes taken out upon a rise of ground to hearten the warriors
making their desperate stand. The Arrows were for power in the center of
a fight and were not to be defiled by the touch of an enemy or fall to earth,
etc. as you know.

   Of course, there was no printed ritual and dogma to preserve the exact
procedures during the change from agrarian life to one of pure hunting,
with the horse and iron and powder, all absent from the old rituals, or
through the further changes caused by the shrinking buffalo, the sale of
lands, the need to come humbly to another people for goods from 1850
on. These must have brought modification on the rituals and practices,
and left different ideas of the procedures with different people, depending
upon the time of their information. Certainly nothing that came into the
presence of the Arrows or the Hat should have been touched by iron or
powder. For a long time as I recall now, everything used in ceremonials of
either sacred object had to be from back in the old age Cheyenne country.
Practically everything except the food. The use of Plains silver sage on
the ground in any of the ceremonies was condemned by the Old ones as
late as 1800. Oak bark, leaves, and acorns once had important places in
Cheyenne ceremonials, I understand.

2. It was 1875 that the Arrows were brought north and not 1876, for there
were no troops in the Kansas and south Nebraska regions to intercept the
Cheyennes in 1876. The Red Cloud agent reported this flight of southern
Cheyennes north in 1875, verifying the stories of the Indians and the buffalo hunters at Cheyenne Hole on the Sappa.

3. For one overall white man version of the attack on the Cheyennes March
17, 1876, see "Statement by Col. J.J. Reynolds to the Department Com-
mander concerning the Charges Against him, March 28, 1876, Dept. of
the Platte Document Files Letters Received 1876 War Records, National
Archives, Washington DC" and in same files, December 7, 1876 "Sub-
poenas for General Court Martial against Col. J.J. Reynolds and Captain
Alexander Moore, to report to Cheyenne Jan. 5, 1877." The 22 witnesses

included both Bats [Big Bat Pourier and Little Bat], Provost, and Grourard. The records of the entire general court martial proceedings are available.

————

MARCH 6, 1964

Gene Price
Marathon Oil Company, Public Relations,
Findlay, Ohio, 45840

Dear Gene Price:
Thanks for the word on the *Outdoor Nebraska* article. [. . .]
About White Clay [Nebraska]: There's a lot of scattered material on the Extension as it's called, in my files and elsewhere but so far as I know it has never been brought together. Check with the Nebraska State Historical Society for evidence of the rumor that Theodore Roosevelt filed on a homestead there when the strip was opened to filings. (Federal Land Office Records have been returned to the states where ever the facilities for their preservation and use were good.) Give the legal description of the Extension, which was, as you will know, created to keep bootleggers from too close roots to the Pine Ridge Agency.[18] Naturally it became a camp for them. For the old race track and gathering ground see my *Cattlemen*, page 410, etc.
Good luck,

————

JULY 27, 1964

Richard W. Baron, Publisher,
The Dial Press
750 Third Ave.
New York, NY 10017

Dear Mr. Baron:
I am sorry that even the Foreword of *Little Big Man* gives me the uncomfortable sense of pity for an author who must shout his maleness to the world as the *Esquire* article about Big Caroline produced. One might like to think this shouting satirical, but it's just too obvious and pathetic for that, its premise too faulty.

I Do Not Apologize

The business about the war bonnets is such a giveaway. First, "the great Crazy Horse" (ix) never owned a war bonnet. All such ornamentation was forbidden by his medicine, as it was for many of the greater Plains warriors. Old Crazy Horse, the war chief's father, had one from his warrior days, and Greasy Head, the dark-skinned Indian who married Crazy Horse's breed widow (and in good Sioux custom took the name of his illustrious predecessor) owned one, as did a couple of the other four men of the name who signed the Sioux Treaty of 1889, twelve years after the Crazy Horse was killed.

Further, war bonnets were not restricted to the overtly male as the author seems to think. Historically there were several women war bonnet owners among both Sioux and Cheyennes, as they were warrior women. As in any matrilineal society, the woman's line is the important one and when men of council chieftain qualities in a band grew scarce, women might be elected to the chieftainships. Sitting Bull had two among the various bands he brought back from Canada in 1881, because the Sioux wars had decimated the ranks of young men with potentialities. One of these had been a warrior woman—with a war bonnet.

When a man became a real chieftain, a council chief, he wore only the one feather of his office, usually in an erect position at the back of his head.

[. . .] One of the handsomest Sioux war bonnets, with two tails that trailed on the ground behind, belonged to Pipe, the famous Minneconjou Sioux berdache.[19]

Certainly the Cheyennes would have loved Big Caroline. As a minority people they welcomed practically any woman to the tribe, the bigger the better. They had a woman warrior in both the Rosebud and the Custer battles—women of convincing size and bravery. By the Plains matrilineal systems, the Cheyennes could get no women from other peoples except by capture or adoption. This could have been such an amusing book, sorry.

2.
Political
Activism /
Social Justice
for the
Tribes

———

I   n the 1950s, as her career reached a notable level of success, San-
     doz became more intense in her political activism on behalf of the
     Northern Cheyenne tribe after witnessing firsthand the appalling
conditions under which the people were living on the reservation in Montana. Always cognizant of the political climate in the United States, Sandoz
kept abreast of current events and held a mix of political views. Like most
Americans, she was conservative on some issues and liberal on others; still
Sandoz always considered herself a staunch liberalist and almost invariably
took the side of the "underdog." But in the 1950s, she became increasingly
astute in criticizing federal Indian policy. She very quickly saw most of the
legislation for what it was: a strategy to detribalize all Native peoples, assimilate them into the greater American populace, and divest them of their land
bases. A particular target of her disdain was the dual policies of termination
and relocation. The history of these policies is pertinent to the discussion
here, and a bit of explanation is in order.

Simply put, termination was federal Indian policy instituted in the late
1940s through the 1950s as a way to end the U.S. government's responsibilities to American Indian tribes. Its goal was the total assimilation of Native
Americans into the mainstream American population. Historian John Wunder writes that all tribes were scheduled for termination and that no legal ex-
ceptions were to be made: ". . . the trust was over. Federal services were to be
stopped. Reservations were to be abolished. Tribal assets no longer existed."[1]
Many historians and scholars still debate exactly when termination began,
and some think the roots of this policy extend back to the Indian New Deal
policies of the Franklin D. Roosevelt administration,[2] though one could argue
that the seeds of this policy germinated with the Dawes Severalty Act of 1887.

Headed up by the newly appointed commissioner of Indian Affairs, John Collier, the Indian Reorganization Act came into law in 1934, as a reform measure to give American Indians some modicum of self-determination. This act limited the influence of religious education on reservations, replaced the disastrous allotment system, and encouraged tribes to organize their own governmental councils (based on a U.S. model). Collier's goal for the Indian New Deal was to preserve Native American culture and expand their economic opportunities. But even as the Native people seemed to be making some tentative inroads against the negative effects of paternalism, there were distant rumblings of dissent and backlash among western congressmen—both Republicans and Democrats. This dissension, coupled with the entrance of American forces into World War II, began to grow in volume and intensity. At the end of the war, with the resignation of Collier in 1945, the forces behind termination policy and the assimilationists gained ground quickly.

In 1947, the year that Sandoz's politically themed novel *The Tom-Walker* was published, American Indian Affairs experienced significant changes in emerging policy. Republicans and conservative Democrats who held the majority in Congress began severely cutting government expenditures, and first on the chopping block were appropriations for American Indian reservations, as well as monies for the Bureau of Indian Affairs (BIA) payrolls. Arthur V. Watkins, a new Republican senator from Utah, who was unusually zealous when it came to Indian policy, spearheaded the push for termination.[3] Later, with Watkins's appointment to the Indian Claims Commission in 1960, American Indian sovereignty would suffer exponentially as he continued to push termination policy action, ensuring that the federal government would not have to award the Native claimants justly. Watkins would prove to be one of the most forceful proponents of termination policy, and he defended his position on this for the rest of his life. But there were other virulent terminationists among western congressmen and politicos as well, including Wesley D'Ewart (Montana), Patrick McCarran (Nevada), Hugh Butler (Nebraska), and E. Y. Berry (South Dakota). These men knew that the rich resources and land bases of several western tribes would be available for consumption if termination went forward, and they made every effort to assist in that endeavor. Each of these office holders would receive a lengthy letter from Sandoz regarding their positions on termination of the tribes, and voicing her concern about and aversion to the policy.

Public Law 280 was another legislative move that Sandoz realized would cripple American Indian sovereignty during the 1950s. This law removed

Gertrude (Bordeaux) Little Thunder and Mari Sandoz at a book fair, c. late 1950s or early 1960s. Caroline Sandoz Pifer Collection, Mari Sandoz High Plains Heritage Center—Chadron State College. 2003.001.00045.

criminal and civil jurisdiction from the Indian courts and from federal employees in supervisory positions on the reservations, and then handed the jurisdiction over to the state governments. Congress mandated some states to take over, with only a precious few reservations exempted. Other states had an optional opportunity to take over jurisdictions, though some had to amend their constitutions in order to do so.[4] Sandoz knew that this radical legal change was ordered without the consent or even consultation of the Native Americans themselves. Signed into law by President Dwight D. Eisenhower, despite his own apprehension, Public Law 280 would wreak havoc on several reservations, especially in the western states. In Sandoz's home state of Nebraska, for example, the Omahas and Winnebagos saw a dramatic increase in violent crime on their respective reservations. The state law enforcement officials proved unresponsive, and most often turned a blind eye toward the dangerous situation. Luckily, some tribes, like the Lakotas of South Dakota, managed to pass a referendum "revoking the state's legislative attempt to as-

I Do Not Apologize

sert jurisdiction."[5] Nevertheless, Public Law 280 seriously undermined tribal governments. The most damaging termination legislation, including House Concurrent Resolution 108 and PL 280, were signed into law in August 1953, passing with little or no debate, "cloaked among a series of minor bills."[6] As the letters will show, Sandoz felt certain the adverse effects of termination on American Indian nations would be harsh and long lasting.

While termination policy began its devastation on tribal sovereignty and tribes as a whole, "relocation projects" began their work on Native American individuals. Sandoz lobbied hard against relocation, knowing these plans would be another ploy to divest Native people of their tribal land bases. Of their own volition, American Indians from many tribes had been relocating for several years to urban centers and smaller towns to work, especially after World Wars I and II, although the numbers were never great. However, as federal Indian policy, the Voluntary Relocation Program began in earnest in 1952, directed by Dillon S. Meyer. Interestingly, part of Meyer's unique qualification for the position was his "successful" directorship of the Japanese internment camps during World War II.[7] First cousin to termination policy, the relocation program was created and heavily promoted by the BIA to entice young Native people to move from the reservations to large urban centers with the promise of job training, secure job placements, good housing, health benefits, and a chance to become upwardly mobile with a new life in mainstream American society. Some of the best and brightest American Indians were recruited with the offer of a one-way bus ticket to an urban relocation center—perhaps Chicago, Salt Lake City, Denver, Dallas, or San Francisco—provided with a month's rent and a few amenities to start their new lives. Soon they found themselves far from home, on their own, in the large industrialized urban landscape. While a fortunate few prospered, for the majority of young Natives, the dream of a new life in the city most often proved to be a nightmarish existence. There were several problems with the Voluntary Relocation Program. First of all, it was not all that "voluntary." The BIA actively enlisted Native Americans for the program, and the propaganda was slick and alluring. Pamphlets and brochures depicted prospering, well-adjusted Native families living in the cities, and these were liberally distributed among the poorest reservations.[8] The enticement was successful, and each year the numbers of young Native Americans who applied for the program increased.

The realities relocatees confronted when they arrived at their destinations in the urban centers were vastly different than what they had expected. Conditions were generally very bad: only cursory job training was provided, minimum- or below-minimum-wage jobs or seasonal jobs were often the only ones available, health benefits were nonexistent, tenement housing was located in urban ghettos, and rampant racial discrimination flourished. Culture shock, too, disheartened and depressed many relocated Native people. Adjusting to the new urban landscape—crowds, asphalt and concrete covering much of the earth, clocks everywhere, elevators, teeming noisy traffic—proved difficult for many who had come from rural, remote reservations with little or no education or coping skills in regard to these things. Wilma Mankiller, former principal chief of the Oklahoma Cherokees, writes of her relocation experiences as a youngster:

> The noises of the city, especially at night, were bewildering. We had left behind the sounds of roosters, dogs, coyotes, bobcats, owls, crickets, and other animals moving through the woods. We knew the sounds of nature. Now we heard traffic and other noises that were foreign. The police and ambulance sirens were the worst. That very first night in the big city, we were all huddled under the covers. . . . I thought it was some sort of wild creature screaming.[9]

Far from their supportive community and family members, Native American relocatees began to succumb to homesickness and despair, and rather than becoming "upwardly mobile," many found themselves in a downward spiral of depression. Many gave up and returned to the reservations, most of these emotionally and financially poorer than when they had originally set out for the cities. Sandoz witnessed this devastation firsthand and it broke her heart.

A small percentage of Native relocatees tenaciously managed to make progress in the urban areas, especially those with good educations or those who had worked in the cities before or during World War II. One form of support and community came in the shape of intertribal "Indian Centers" in many of the urban locations—a focal point that helped families survive and adjust in the cities. The relocation program was not especially successful for helping American Indians assimilate into mainstream America as planned; rather, it proved most often to be detrimental for young Native people, costly to the American government, and was eventually halted in the 1970s. However, in 1966, when Mari Sandoz died, relocation was ongoing.

Neither termination nor relocation fully accomplished what it was designed to do—end the federal trust with the tribes and assimilate American Indians into the dominant society. However, these policies had direct and calamitous effects on several tribes. The Wisconsin Menominees and the Oregon Klamaths, for example, were both relatively prosperous and self-sufficient before termination significantly damaged them.[10] Early targets for termination, they found themselves in dire straits almost immediately after the bills passed through congress. Both tribes found their forests under siege and, without federal protections and management, easily available for uncontrolled cutting. Sandoz, who for several years taught a summer writing course at the University of Wisconsin–Madison, saw some of the results of this wastefulness, and decried it. The Menominees tried delaying tactics against the termination process and eventually had some success, but this strategy was not without serious consequences. During the delays, with their services cut and the treaty rights splintered, many Menominees had to seek state assistance and sank into poverty. It would be several years before the tribe recovered and reestablished federal recognition. The Klamaths also tried to resist termination after the wheels had been set in motion. Seriously factionalized with internal conflicts over the offer of per capita payments for their assets, the Klamaths lost a substantial portion of their forest to private owners.[11] When the Watters commission and conservationists finally realized that by opening the Klamath forest to unlimited cutting, the lumber market would become saturated (and drive market prices down significantly), implementation of the original termination bill was scrapped. With legal assistance, the Klamaths began to seek reinstatement for federal recognition, gaining ground in the 1970s and finally reaching their goal in 1986; but the damage was done. What was left of their forest land is still held in federal trust. The Klamaths are still in litigation to retrieve portions of their forests, a process that seems unending.

Sandoz was concerned for all tribes, but especially for the Northern Cheyennes. Although they were not on the list for those to be terminated immediately, the Northern Cheyennes were still at risk and being directly affected by limited land sales. Fortunately, they were able to stop the sale of the Bixby tract, a valuable land and water resource that was under consideration for sale as a result of termination. But as the correspondence illuminates, cuts in federal services remained a stressor for the majority of tribal members. The closing of their hospital on the reservation was extremely disconcerting for the Northern Cheyennes, as health care was of great concern.

Approximately one hundred tribes were negatively impacted one way or another before termination policy fell out of favor in 1962. The formal dismantlement of termination did not occur until the Nixon administration, well after the time of Sandoz's death. The aftershocks of both termination

Mari Sandoz on Arabian steeds at the Lazy VV Ranch near Nederland, Colorado. Sandoz went to the Van Vleet ranch for several summers during the 1940s to ride and write. Caroline Sandoz Pifer Collection, Mari Sandoz High Plains Heritage Center—Chadron College. 2003.001.00102 and 2003.001.00504.

and relocation are still being felt, and the damages and losses from these policies are impossible to assess accurately. The BIA concealed relocation records, for example, and abandoned keeping statistics as criticism grew during the latter years of the program.[12]

The hardships and agony that Native Americans experienced because of these twin policies will not soon be forgotten. N. Scott Momaday's 1968 Pulitzer Prize winning novel, *House Made of Dawn*, graphically relates the effects of relocation. The book, still in print, is a staple of American Indian literature and taught widely in both high school and college classrooms. Since 1968, other Native writers, musicians, and artists have chronicled vivid stories of "urban Indians" (a term coined from the program of relocation itself). Powerful poems and stories by such noted Native writers as Joy Harjo, Wendy Rose, John Trudell, and Sherman Alexie explore the themes of relocation experience in the cities. Just as scholars and historians debate the roots of termination policy, so too do they continue discussion and examination of the lasting effects these programs have on Native Americans today. Sandoz was correct in her assessment of these programs as a permanent blemish on America's ideas of "justice for all."

The ways in which politics and governmental policies affected the tribes remained a troublesome and frustrating situation for Sandoz for many years. Although she sometimes felt defeated in her quest to get legislators to pay attention to and honor the treaty rights of American Indians, she never gave up the fight for justice entirely. As the record will show, she searched for alternative venues in which to inform the American public of the crisis in American Indian affairs. Such venues included television and radio, where Sandoz spoke at some length regarding the conditions in Indian country. She managed a guest appearance on the popular game show *Strike It Rich* as a contestant, and won 120 dollars in prize money, which she promptly sent to the Cheyenne Day School in Birney, Montana. She suggested to the instructors that the money be spent on art supplies and athletic equipment for the students. The sum, significant in the early 1950s, was augmented by other donations to the Cheyenne school children at Birney that Sandoz received from concerned citizens as a result of her television appearance. Although the amounts of money were not grand or impressive, Sandoz knew that every little bit could benefit the school children on the reservation.

Sandoz took advantage of many opportunities to remain active on behalf of the tribes, but in these actions, she tried not to overstep the boundaries of respect. Sandoz believed that Native American people were perfectly capable of handling their own lives and affairs if given the opportunity to do so. She consulted with tribal chairmen and spoke with the people themselves to see where her action and assistance could be of the most help—she did not rush in to impose her own agenda. As the letters reveal, Sandoz became actively involved in American Indian affairs to seek social justice and fair treatment for the tribal people of her region and beyond.

MARCH 31, 1944

Elaine Goodale Eastman
319 Elm Street
North Hampton, Mass.

Dear Elaine Goodale Eastman

I am so ashamed that so much time has lapsed since I received your most welcome letter. Unfortunately I was in a book and somehow I can't seem to come out of the sort of trance I go into when I start writing until I have down what must be said. I think you will understand. Your work has a special sort of dedication to it, so you probably retreat even further from the immediate world.

About the Indians: In the past, I've kept myself rather aloof from the various white man-Indian movements because so many of them wish to do this or that for the Indian to "improve" him. Such movements seem to me incredibly arrogant. What the Indians need I think, is freedom from the hamperings—economic, political, cultural, and spiritual—that the white man has put upon him. It breaks my heart to see the young Indian have to deny his individuality, his whole heritage and try to become indistinguishable from the whites so he can make a decent living.

We've had many young Sioux working in the ranch country. My sister and her husband have had several. Flora felt grieved that these boys kept silent under the taunting from the more ignorant whites around who ridiculed them because when they had been well educated they returned to their people. Yet there was no criticism of Flora, who with a degree in botany, returned to run the orchard place of Old Jules.

When I get my book off, I'll look into the Indian matter again. Surely something *must* be done. I hope the coming spring finds you your own vigorous self.

Sincerely,

———

SEPTEMBER 9, 1949

Van Vleets[13]
Nederland, CO

Dear Boss and Rose:

Just a bit of a report on the goings on and on Harold Rhodenbaugh. [. . .]

At the Custer Battlefield Harold took pictures of me and the headstones, the battleground, and with Superintendent Luce, an old Seventh Cavalry man. Here at Lame Deer he got me with old Chief Gray and his wife, with my typewriter on my knee and a lot of big-eyed Indian children watching, and me at the Tongue River roundup camp, with my knee on a Cheyenne steer, using the needle, etc. If there are no good ones it won't be Harold's fault. Yesterday evening the men started back to Jackson and I'm settled down in the hospital here, empty because of the 1947 economy drive that cut off the Cheyenne hospital appropriations, and for the doctor, too. Apparently the 1400 Cheyennes here are to remain well until Congress feels generous, although by treaty right they are to have both hospital and doctor facilities on the agency. Unfortunately there have been several unavoidable deaths here recently, and much needless suffering—including two complicated deliveries that had to be taken with only Indian midwives along, to the Crow hospital over fifty miles of rutted night roads. There's not even a drug store here. And then some complain that the old Indians are returning to the spell of the medicine men.

But enough—the sun is bright, the chiefs are coming in for a meeting about the range cooperative and the young people are gay and handsome and feel well. The language of the old, even of old Sand Crane, keeper of the Sacred Hat, the sacred emblem of the old Cheyennes, is musical and liquid, although the old man is blind and bedfast and on old age pension of some kind.

My contacts are working out pleasantly here; I may not be back for two weeks.

Love,

————

OCTOBER 18, 1949

President Harry Truman
Washington, D.C.

Dear Mr. President:

Last night a long time friend, Otho DeVilbiss, Public Relations, BPOE, stopped in. He told me of his very pleasant visit at the White House last summer with the winner of the Elks' Americanism Essay Contest, and of your interest in the American Indian, and your extensive reading on the subject, including my book, *Crazy Horse*.

I am happy to hear all this, and regret I did not know it earlier. I have just returned from an extensive cover of the old Plains Indian country, particularly the Tongue River Reservation of the Northern Cheyennes, where the calamities of the present compelled me to shift my interest from the old buffalo hunting days to the problems of the present.

After the appalling storms of last winter, the Reservation was struck by a devastating drouth this summer, followed by grasshoppers that destroyed even the small gardens. With no railroad and no good roads, hay costs around forty dollars a ton laid down on the reservation, so the tribal herds, in which the Cheyennes took so much pride, are having to be sold down far below even what survived last winter. This seems a final defeat to these people; one more defeat that the sons of the old fighting Cheyennes have to accept without a fight. During the last few years they had to see their agency discontinued, their reservation combined with that of their hereditary enemies, the Crows, and worse, see their new hospital stand closed, so the sick, the old of the 1,800 people, many with tuberculosis, active or incipient, have to be hauled over the rough or snowbound roads to the already over-crowded hospital of the Crows. I went to see old Sand Crane, Keeper of the Medicine Hat, once as sacred an object to the Northern Cheyennes as the Cross of Christ would be to the Christian. He lay in a one room log hut, blind and bedfast. Could he be persuaded to go to die even in physical comfort among the Crows?

The situation, Mr. President, is very bad. The people are discouraged, resentful. It is true that they get small jobs, such as beet topping down in Wyoming, and so on, but seldom more than a few days. Their agency, too, has been re-opened last year, with a good experienced man, Superintendent Hunter, in charge. But there is almost nothing from which the Indians can make a living. And always they reminded me of the hospital, closed, empty, a symbol of rejection by another economy-minded Congress that cut the appropriation of the small tribe of Cheyennes, as congresses have been doing since the 1850s. Back in the old days they could go out to hunt buffalo, join the hostile Sioux in their wars of protest, cost the government millions for the thousands congress saved. Now they must be grateful for every name that they can get on the relief rolls. It is not good to see these people on relief, descendants of a tribe that produced some of the greatest warriors of the Plains, their women among the finest quill and bead workers, women considered by both whites and Indians as the most virtuous of any people on the continent.

I went to Billing to the Regional Offices of the Indian Service to protest the plight of the Cheyennes and was told there was no money to open the hospital, or apparently, for the means of a livelihood that, I am told by Superintendent Hunter and his staff, could be opened to the Cheyennes.

For, Mr. President, these Indians need not be in such straits even with all the forces of the elements against them. There is much work that needs to be done on the Reservation. First of all, everyone agrees, there should be a good highway. That would make work for many able-bodied men for a time. Then, in addition to the dream and hope of oil in the future, there is the immediate actuality of considerable timber, and a thirty foot surface vein of coal of good commercial quality. The Indians have a little saw mill going, and a small mine, enough to fill the local demand. With a good highway, some financing, and a training program in lumbering, mining, and marketing, these Indians can once more become the independent, self-reliant people they were when they cost the United States government so much in money and lives to conquer.

I do not apologize for the length of this letter. I feel very strongly on what is happening to the Northern Cheyennes. I am certain you would feel as strongly if you had seen what I saw this summer.

Now to happier business. I am sending you an autographed copy of *Crazy Horse*. And if Margaret happens to be down in the Village and has a moment to spare, I'd like to have her drop in. I understand she had an uncle in Denver, my favorite town—

Faithfully yours,

————

JANUARY 31, 1950

Association on American Indian Affairs,
48 East 86ᵗʰ Street,
New York, N.Y.

Gentlemen:

If you have the names of the committees on Indian Affairs in the present Congress, I should like the list.

I want to intercede for the Northern Cheyennes, with the hope of getting some betterment in the really desperate situation. I was up on the agency at Lame Deer some weeks last fall, and I came away appalled at what was happening to these people. I have written to President Truman, etc., and I went up to Billings to the regional offices there on my way back from Montana. But everywhere I get the same reply: it is the fault of the economy minded congress of 1947.

The Cheyenne wars were the result, in a large measure, of economy-minded congresses, saving thousands while spending millions. Now the Cheyennes can't go on the warpath, although I should be tempted to do so, if I were a Cheyenne of the Tongue River now.

Thank-you for the list—

————

[Attached to letter]

Indian Affairs in the House of Representatives are referred to the Subcommittee on Indian Affairs of the Committee on Public Lands.

Members of this Subcommittee are:

Toby Morris,
    Chairman   of Oklahoma
John R. Murdock   of Arizona
Compton I. White   of Idaho
Walter S. Baring   of Nevada
Reva Beck Bosone   of Utah
Fred Marshall   of Minnesota
William Lemke   of North Dakota
Frank A. Barrett   of Wyoming
Wesley A. D' Ewart   of Montana
Norris Poulson   of California
J. Hardin Peterson   of Florida
E.L. Bartlett   of Alaska

Indian Affairs in the Senate are referred to the Committee on Interior and Insular Affairs.

Members of this Committee are:

Joseph C. O'Mahoney,
    Chairman   of Wyoming
James E. Murray   of Montana
Sheridan Downey   of California
Ernest W. McFarland   of Arizona
Clinton P. Anderson   of New Mexico
Glen H. Taylor   of Idaho
Herbert H. Lehman   of New York
Hugh Butler   of Nebraska
Eugene D. Milliken   of Colorado
Guy Gordon   of Oregon
Zales N. Ecton   of Montana
George W. Malone   of Nevada
Arthur V. Watkins   of Utah

Dear Margaret Marshall:[14]

While down in Washington a few days ago I was told by some people from the Lame Deer Agency that a couple of magazine men were there some weeks ago. So that's covered, for good or ill. It's probably from your energetic efforts. Thank you.

As you will know, the thermometer's been down towards fifty below along the Tongue river this winter, and the 700 buffalo the newspapers reported were given to the Cheyennes turned out to be seven buffaloes and twelve or thirteen elk—for the boarding school.

I'm working on the men who can help restore the Cheyenne appropriations, and do something about helping utilize the natural resources on the agency. Perhaps nothing will come of it. It's hell to be a minority. But we keep hoping . . .

Sincerely,

———

FEBRUARY 4, 1950

Representative Wesley A. D'Ewart[15]
The House of Representatives
Washington, D.C.

Dear Mr. D'Ewart:

May I say a word in behalf of the Northern Cheyenne Indians on the Tongue River Reservation in your state? You, more than perhaps any other man in public life, must be disturbed by what has been happening to these people.

Last fall I spent some weeks on the reservation, finishing the research on my Cheyenne Indian book, which covers the pre-agency period and is to be a companion piece to my Sioux biography, *Crazy Horse*. However, the calamities of the present compelled me to shift my interest from the old buffalo hunting days to the problems of the present.

As you will know, after the appalling storms of the winter of 1948–49, the Reservation was struck by a devastating drouth last summer, followed by grasshoppers that destroyed even the small gardens. With no railroad and no good roads, hay costs around forty dollars a ton laid down on the reservation, so the tribal herds, in which the Cheyennes took so much pride, had to be sold down far below even what survived the preceding winter. This seems a final defeat to these people; one more defeat that the sons of the old fighting Cheyennes have to accept without a fight. During the last few years they had to see their agency discontinued, their reservation combined with that of their hereditary enemies, the Crows, and worse, see their new hospital stand closed, so that the sick, the old of these 1,800 people, many with tuberculosis, active or incipient, have to be hauled over the rough or snowbound roads to the already over-crowded hospital of the Crows. I went to see old Sand Crane, Keeper of the Medicine Hat, as sacred an object to the Northern Cheyennes as the Cross of Christ would be to a Christian. He lay in a one room log hut, blind and bedfast. Could he be persuaded to go to die even in physical comfort among the Crows?

The situation is really very bad. The people are discouraged, resentful, and now very hungry. I don't see how they exist. It is true that they got small jobs last fall, such as beet topping down in Wyoming, and so on, but seldom more than a few days. Their agency, too, has been reopened the last year, with a good, experienced man, Superintendent Hunter, in charge. But there is almost nothing from which the Indians can make a living. And always they remind me of the hospital, closed, empty, a symbol of rejection by a congress—trying to economize where there would be least protest—that cut the appropriations of the small tribe of Cheyennes, as congresses have been doing since the 1850s. Back in the old days these Indians could go out to hunt buffalo, join the hostile Sioux in their wars of protest, cost the government millions for the thousands that were saved. Now they must be grateful for every name that can get on the relief rolls. It is not good to see these people on relief—descendants of a tribe that produced some of the greatest warriors of the Plains, their women among the finest quill and bead workers, women considered by both whites and Indians as the most virtuous of any people on the continent.

I went to Billings to the Regional Offices of the Indian Service to protest the plight of the Cheyennes and was told that there was no money to do anything, not for the hospital or to develop any of the means for livelihood that I am told by Superintendent Hunter and his staff could be opened to the Cheyennes.

I was all over the reservation; I talked to many people and I am convinced that these Indians need not be in such straits, even with all of the forces of the elements against them. There is much work that needs to be done on the Reservation. First of all, everyone agrees, there should be a good highway. That would make work for any able bodied men for a time.

Then, in addition of the dream and hope of oil in the future, there is the immediate actuality of some timber for building, and particularly, it seems to me, for the study of forestry. The Cheyenne veteran seems to have no on-the-job training available, and I wonder why. Then there is a 30 foot service vein of coal of good commercial quality. The Indians have a small mine going, enough to fill the local demand. With a good highway, some financing, and a training program in lumbering, mining and marketing, these Indians could once more become the independent, self-reliant people they were when they cost the United States government so much in money and in lives to conquer.

I do not apologize for the length of this letter. I feel very strongly on what is happening to the Northern Cheyennes. I grew up around the Sioux of Pine Ridge, South Dakota, where there are still some Cheyennes inter-married, and I have been on the Tongue River Reservation many times. Never have these people seemed so hopeless, so defeated. I know you are aware of this situation, but I am wondering what any of us can do.

Yours respectfully,

––––––

FEBRUARY 4, 1950

Superintendent John G. Hunter,
Tongue River Agency,
Lame Deer, Montana

Dear Mr. Hunter:

Can you send Margaret Marshall, *The Nation*, 20 Vesey St., New York, N. Y., material on the situation of the Northern Cheyennes immediately? She would like to have information on the points mentioned in my letter to President Truman, and in addition, something on the disturbance and threat of the oil promoters, if there is no policy objection. Send anything else you have in mind.

Margaret Marshall is particularly anxious to do something about this attempt to defraud the Indians in their desperate need. She was graduated from Missoula, and feels a kinship for the region, in addition to her natural allegiance to all the needy people of the world. She wants to do a quick, pointed editorial on the immediate situation, so copies can be rushed to the congressmen and senators.

We have put out a letter to the committees in charge of Indian Affairs in the senate and the house of representatives the last few days, my typist and I, about the Cheyennes. If you can think of any others who should have a little nudge on the elbow, let me know.

Best wishes,

———

APRIL 15, 1950

Mr. Rufus Wallowing
Everett Hotel,
Washington, D.C.

Dear Mr. Wallowing:

I am grieved to hear that the Cheyennes are still in such an unhappy state, but pleased that your old-time Cheyenne courage is carrying on through the fight.

I wish I could have received your letter a couple of weeks ago. I called a few good people in Washington since the letter arrived this morning, but everyone seems to be out of town. I'll try again Monday. In the meantime I sent your letter with some notes I made from your material in the Miles City paper and from Mr. Hunter's files to Margaret Marshall of *The Nation*, a weekly magazine. I wrote for the material for her long ago, but I can see that with the investigation and so on in progress up there, Mr. Hunter was not free to send me what I wanted. I regret this removal of Superintendent Hunter very much.

In addition to the material to Miss Marshall, I sent a note over to Mr. Lesser, Association on American Indian Affairs, 48 East 86th Street, New York, hoping he can interest some newspaper men here in your difficulties. Publicity is always good for these things. I've given both Mr. Lesser and Miss Marshall your hotel address in Washington. If you can come to New York, will you call me as soon as you arrive? I'm in the telephone book. I hope my letting *The Nation* see your letter was not unwise. I considered it carefully, and there seemed nothing confidential.

This winter I sent modifications of my letter to President Truman to the heads of the subcommittees on Indian affairs in both houses of Congress as well as to other members of the committees who might be particularly interested and make good use of the information. The response to the letters has been excellent, but I know politicians talk out of both sides of their mouths.

I have been unable to return to Lame Deer this winter as I hoped, but some of the pictures taken last summer will appear in an article about me in the June issue of *Flair*. I'll send you a copy. There is one of Chief Ed Gray and his wife, one of the vaccinating in the cow camp, and one of you and me beside the frame of the sweat lodge in the Gray yard. The article is not by me, so I doubt if there will be much about Indians in it, but the pictures will be there. The rest taken last summer are to be saved for an article I plan to do when the immediate pressures of the Cheyenne book and other things are off.

I wish you and the Cheyennes the very best of successes in your efforts here in the east,

———

APRIL 15, 1950

Alexander Lesser, Executive Director,
Association on American Indian Affairs, Inc.
48 East 86ᵗʰ Street,
New York 28, N.Y.

Dear Mr. Lesser,

I am enclosing a copy of a letter from Rufus Wallowing, president of the Tribal Council, Northern Cheyenne, also a copy of some notes I took from the file on the subject of his letter. The original I am sending to Margaret Marshall of *The Nation*. We have been trying to get this material for some time for an editorial for the magazine but there have been the usual delays. I knew the story but I had to have authority to use it. It may be too late for Miss Marshall, but I hope not.

The point that Mr. Wallowing doesn't mention in his letter is that legitimate oil companies can deal direct with the Indian bureau for oil rights. What he can't mention is the bribing of the tribal council members that was going on when I was up there; not that I could swear to this . . .

You know the technique for removing the supervisory powers for the Secretary of the Interior. With enough bribery in the council and enough hunger among the people they can get the required 2/3 adult vote. Then, as the ex-GIs kept reminding me, all the tribal property can be even given away, if the council was so minded, and with it the little hope those young men had for a future for their children. The lease, the Indians told me, is for $100,000 immediate cash payment. It must look pretty big by now, with winter still on up there, no matter what the rights sold for that sum—a little over fifty dollars for each Indian.

I realize that this is out of your field, but just any little bit of publicity might help Rufus. He is one of the few men, mixed blood or full blood, up there who have had any college work at all, and you can see how pitifully little his short time at Carlisle did him. But he is a stubborn man, and so he keeps up this desperate fight. He is of the old Two Moons family, of the family that fought so bravely against Custer beside the Sioux on the Little Big Horn.

Do you suppose the *New York Herald* might be interested in a little about him if he comes to New York?

———

MAY 8, 1950

Wilbert B. Harvey
Birney Day School
Birney, Montana

Dear W. Harvey:

Can you send me the full name and address of Mr. Beatty in Washington that you mentioned in your letter? Unless you think it might harm your project there, I should like to write him. I can, through my Cheyenne work, my short camping around Birney twenty years ago, and my visit with Sand Crane last fall and the picture and stories from Edward, do this without involving the Harveys at all. I can make a good case, I think, that the young people like Edward have a right to the best possible opportunities, without involving you in insubordination.

Or can you suggest anything better, or in addition?

Tell Edward Sand Crane I shall return his stories as soon as I've had time to study them some more, and I'll have my typist make him several copies in type, too, so in case one gets lost, he'll still have others. I hope that he will collect more material. He can, with this start, become a historian and artist for his people as the old Cheyenne picture writers were. It will take hard work and strong belief in the old Cheyenne virtues of courage, honesty and self-denial, but he comes from a great family and has, I suspect, the makings of a modern Cheyenne very fit to stand beside his ancestors.

I had the material contained in his stories, but I am going to use his name, with his grandfather's as an additional reference for the story of Custer's lie in the Sacred Arrow Lodge.

About your shy, unaggressive Cheyenne girls: modesty is, as you know, an old, old Cheyenne virtue, but that doesn't mean that all Cheyenne women were so withdrawn. As they will know it was a woman, the mother of Tobacco, who brought the system of chieftainships, 4 from each of the ten bands and 4 Old Man chiefs—44, to them. There have been four warrior women among them in historical times, two, Yellow Woman and Buffalo Calf Road, from the Northern Cheyennes, and Mochisi from the south. She was sent to prison in Florida with the 33 Cheyennes for her part in avenging the killing of Cheyennes by illegal buffalo hide hunters. As you know, every minority grows some strong women, see the women of the Old Testament.

But enough—I'm under great pressure on the book, and I have to fly to Nebraska for an honorary doctorate. I hope the Harveys can be saved for Birney.

Sincerely,

———

JUNE 27, 1950

Dr. William Walcott Beatty, Director,
Education, Bureau of Indian Affairs,
Washington, D. C.

Dear Doctor Beatty:
Sometime in April I wrote you from out west and the letter was mailed in a snowstorm at a rural route box. None of the other letters mailed there that day ever arrived at their destination and I presume that yours was also lost.

I wrote about the Northern Cheyennes on the Tongue River Reservation, particularly at Birney. When I was finishing up my final round of field work on my double biography of Little Wolf and Dull Knife last fall, I went to see Sand Crane, the old Keeper of the Sacred Buffalo Hat. Through this and some subsequent correspondence I became interested in the school at Birney, particularly in such pupils as Edward Sand Crane, who is already a good artist and, despite his language handicap, writes well the stories of the old Cheyennes who submerged their egos in the good of their people. He is, I think, the kind of talented descendant one might expect of the old time Cheyennes.

Yet this flowering at Birney is, I think, due largely to the Harveys, the teachers in the two teacher school. Being Indian, Mrs. Harvey has been able to break through the current tendency of the Cheyennes to withdraw, a tendency evident to me when I returned there last September and October. The friendliness to his wife made it possible for Mr. Harvey, whom I knew at the University of Wisconsin two years ago . . . , to bring out the creative aspects of the Cheyennes' temperament.

This is not, understand, a plea for the Harveys. They don't need that. But if Birney is reduced to a one teacher school, as the pupils write me may happen, there will not be time for work with anything except the barest essentials in the three Rs. I've taught five years in one room rural schools; I know.

I am disturbed by what has happened to the Cheyennes in general. Ever since Sumner confiscated their goods from Yellow Horse, the peace man at Bent's Fort in 1857, they have had less than their due. Once they could fight and cost the government millions for the thousands saved by economic moves. Now the Cheyennes can only work their way out of their sad state by enlarged opportunities, economic and educational. Through boys like young Sand Crane they could perhaps once more find the leadership and the pride of peoples they must feel. I hope something can be done.

Thank you,

———

MAY 30, 1951

Superintendent Carl L. Pearson
Northern Cheyenne Agency
Lame Deer, Montana.

Dear Mr. Pearson:

In my campaign to call attention to the plight of the American Indian, particularly the Northern Cheyennes, I wrote a long letter to the N.Y. *Herald Tribune* in the way of additions to what Mr. Durston of Billings wrote. My letter came to the attention of Warren Hull, of CBS radio and TV station. He asked me to send in a short letter about the situation of the Cheyennes and a request to his program, "Strike It Rich," for some special item for these Indians. Yesterday I appeared on the program, used both on TV and radio nationwide. I showed a picture done for me by Edward Sandcrane of Birney Day School some time ago, and made an appeal, energetic if not long or effective, for the Cheyennes. And then, by answering a few easy questions cautiously, won $120.00. This, as I stipulated to Mr. Hull, is to go to the Birney Day School for art supplies and a little addition to their athletic equipment, say, bats and mitts for baseball or basket balls, etc.

I should like to endorse this check over to you, with the stipulation on it that the money is to go to the Birney Day School. Will this work out all right through your office?

I am very happy that we managed to get the Whitney Fellowship for Gerry Harvey. I haven't heard from her so I don't know what her plans are.

Sincerely,

The Ford Foundation
575 Madison Avenue
New York, N. Y.

Gentlemen:

From the *New York Times* of June 3, 1951, I get a fine picture of the tremendous work outlined by the Ford Foundation. I am particularly pleased with the provisions made to facilitate college work for exceptional young people from the high schools. From my annual summer connection with the University of Wisconsin, I know the program there will be well and enthusiastically executed.

Because of my interest in opportunities for young people, and my familiarity with the lack of opportunities for the young American Indians, I wonder if there might not be some provision in your plans for them. The economic situation on most reservations is so bad that few Indians can hope to finance even tuition for their sons and daughters, and the schools are so inadequate that scholarships are practically unavailable to the few who finish high school.

I am enclosing a brief of a talk I gave before the annual meeting of the Association on American Indian Affairs recently, and a subsequent letter published by the *New York Herald*, both of which touch on this subject, among other things.

You are to understand that there is nothing I want for myself in this, beyond the privilege of calling something of the Indian's situation to your attention.

Sincerely,

OCTOBER 1, 1952

Alexander Lesser, Executive Director,
Association on American Indian Affairs, Inc.
48 East 86th Street
New York, N. Y.

Dear Doctor Lesser:

Thank you for your letter of September 30, in which you kindly transmitted the invitation of the Officers and Directors of the Association to become an interim member of the Board of Directors.

I had very reluctantly decided to ignore my better judgment and accept. However, after our talk today I had to realize once more how appalling my ignorance of the current Indian situation really is. I see very clearly that I would have to put in a great deal of study and time to fit myself for the responsibilities of such a directorship. Even the use of my name in such a list would imply that I had made a careful study of the entire field. This would be very difficult. Just now I am taking on increasing obligations to be out of New York, both for books and for an advisorship on a moving picture.

I regret very much that I told Mr. Mantell I might accept a directorship for which I am obviously so unqualified. Forgive me.

Sincerely,

———

APRIL 16, 1953

Mr. Rufus Wallowing,
Lame Deer, Montana

Dear Rufus Wallowing:

I am giving your name to John S. Du Mont of the Du Mont Corporation, Greenfield, Massachusetts. He and John Parsons, a New York attorney, are writing a book on the weapons of the Custer battle. I heard Mr. Parsons give a talk on this almost entirely on the arms of the troops and so I suggested some sources for information on the weapons of the Indians. Now they wish to gather all the information that they can from the Indian side. Mr. Du Mont plans to come up to Lame Deer next summer. These two men are seriously interested in the Indians' side and perhaps, some day, they can be useful to you. I think more men who have influence with the present Congress should be familiar with the situation of the Northern Cheyennes.

This week I have been going over the large map to go into my *Cheyenne Autumn*, which will be published in the fall. As I promised, you will receive one of the first copies published.

Sincerely,

———

Rev. Peter Powell
Nashotah House Seminary,
Nashotah, Wisconsin

Dear Reverend Powell:

Thank you for your fine and most generous letter about *Crazy Horse*. I am happy that you felt something of the power of the man coming through, even through the [view] of another race and another way of life.

Yes, I am sure that the profound mysticism of the Lakotas was not a thing without eternal value. I am sure, too, that many felt this; certainly Father DeSmet did. I once heard an old Oglala tell of a long visit he had with the good Father up north somewhere. The details of the visit are not clear to me now, but the Indian's sense of a communion of the spirit between the old man and himself as a boy has stayed with me all these years.

It's generous of you to place any value at all on my efforts for the present-day Indians and to offer your aid. You will do more in a week for them yourself than I could do in years. But perhaps you will write me how things are with you now and then?

Best wishes in this beginning of a new life for you.

Sincerely,

———

OCTOBER 24, 1953

Mr. Rufus Wallowing
Northern Cheyenne Tribal Council
Lame Deer, Montana

Dear Rufus Wallowing:

My book on the Cheyennes is coming out November 17 and I will send you a copy soon afterward. In the meantime, the publicity department of my publisher wants to know if there are any Cheyennes living in New York, or if any will be here November 17-Dec 1, 1953. They think we could get a Cheyenne on Dave Galloway's television program. There is no pay for this, and the time is short, but there would be opportunity to get in a little about the needs of the Northern Cheyennes because my book is about them, and so for a few days, they are news.

Another thing: there will be various newspaper and radio interviews with me about the book, and I'll have an opportunity to get in a few good licks for the People in the present, if I know just what the situation is now.

Is the hospital still closed? If so, how are the sick cared for?

Is there work on the oil explorations and are the Indians getting oil lease money? If so, is it of any amount?

How are the schools? Can everyone who wants to go through the high school, or is enrollment filled?

Will the people be hungry this winter?

Let me know these things and anything more as soon as possible.

Sincerely,

Carbons to Superintendent Pearson and Wilbert Harvey.

————

NOVEMBER 3, 1953

Superintendent Carl L. Pearson,
Tongue River Reservation,
Lame Deer, Montana,

Dear Mr. Pearson:

I am grateful for the information you sent me on the situation on the Reservation, I realized that the psychological climate wasn't good when I was there in 1949. The Cheyennes scarcely seemed the same people that I saw in 1941, even more hopeless, I thought, than they had been in 1930 and 1931.

Yes, I know J. Donald Adams, have known him for better than eighteen years. His interest in Indians is a recent one, I think, at least as far as saying or writing much about them. But sometimes the enthusiasm of the new convert to a cause can make up for long familiarity. The *Times* has usually been a little less inclined to give space to the problems of the American Indians than the *New York Herald Tribune*, but they have always done well by their reviews of Indian books.

My book shows a clear and, I hope, powerful picture of the long series of injustices to the Northern Cheyennes in historical times. It also shows their courage, their initiative and their dogged determination, right up to the reservation period. I hope it will fire the younger people with the pride I think they have a superior right to feel.

Well, we shall see. I'll send you anything that comes out of the interviews and several copies of the book for the Indians. Can you have someone send me the names of the communities that have something that passes for library facilities, school libraries?

I had hoped that there might be a Cheyenne around town here. There are always several Sioux from out home around New York, going to college, laborers in high steel work for the skyscrapers, and so on. That would get much more space in the papers and more radio time in addition to the television.

Thank-you,

———

NOVEMBER 5, 1953

Gerry Harvey
Taos, New Mexico

Dear Gerry:

I wondered what had become of you, as did so many of the girls at Wisconsin this summer. But it's fine to hear from you and at such length. [. . .]

But about the Cheyennes—It's got out that the Cheyenne situation in the present would reflect on the Republicans in the economy congress of 1947, and reflect on the administration's plans to hand over all the Indian natural resources to private interests at any price they care to pay for them. So the outlets for any real facing up to the situation are suddenly closed. Of course the Cheyennes have to learn to live out in the modern world, but to do that on any workable, humane basis, they have to have better schooling and training. That need, I am informed, is to be soft-pedaled in any interviewing with the newspaper or they won't touch on anything of this.

The radio and television don't go in for controversial material at all, or they would have to give as much time to the opposing side, etc., etc. I'll try to get in some of the things you stress, and that I know in my interviews with old friends here and there on the newspapers. Getting an Indian on the air was a good idea, and would have worked the week it was suggested, but now there has been some investigation into what would be brought out—

If there were a Cheyenne here, who could just walk down to the television station, or take a bus, it would pay, for there would be a chance of getting a few remarks through, but probably nothing beyond that. I still hope to find someone. There are Sioux all around; not one Cheyenne so far. Did you ever know Many Kills of South Dakota? He came wandering up just before I went to Wisconsin last spring.

Thanks for the lengthy list of material. And I'll be looking forward to the finished work of your doctorate. Have you made plans to have it published in full, or at least in part?

Love to Woiche and to Wilbert and to the Sangre de Christos,

———

DECEMBER 10, 1953

Mr. Eugene Fisher,
Head, Northern Cheyenne Tribal Council,
Northern Cheyenne Agency,
Lame Deer, Montana

Dear Mr. Fisher:

Enclosed is a clipping from the *Chicago Tribune* of December 6, 1953. This is from an interview in October before I had any specific, up-to-the-minute information on the situation among the Northern Cheyennes. If I had some good, pointed information on your needs, particularly your hopes and fears for the future of the tribe, I could get more into the paper.

Now there is revived interest and I hope to get a press conference on your situation. Will you write me all you can just as soon as you can?

Reporters always want to know about such items as the means of livelihood.

1. What are the prospects for better ranching and farming conditions?

2. What are the prospects for income from oil, and the development of your coal?

3. What do you think could be done to improve the future of the young Cheyennes? Any suggestions for training for the young people?

4. Are you satisfied with your schools? If not, what can be done?

5. How complete will the shift to state supervision be at your reservation? What is your thinking on this?

I'll appreciate anything you wish to write me.

Thank you,

———

JANUARY 15, 1954

Dora Wright,[16]
6–2202 1721 Helena St.
Madison, Wisconsin.

Dear Dora Wright:

Your letter is a most interesting one, and the enclosure from Father Marion of Saint Labre Mission too. I quoted a paragraph about the poor road and the bleak and impoverished country side from the Father's letter several times.

I can understand you sister's reaction. It's no accident that so few intelligent people could stay in the more remote Indian schools. The Cheyennes are a bright, energetic people when free from the pall of malnutrition and hopelessness, too bright for their situation. You probably know that a large percent of them cannot read and write and many comparatively young people, people who went to school, cannot speak passable English. No wonder they are unable to leave the reservation into passable work and are unable to fight for their rights.

Prior to John Collier's administration protests from teachers and Indians generally had to pass through the agent or they were discarded—or they were actually sent back to him. During the Roosevelt administration conditions improved on the Tongue River reservation. A good, well-equipped hospital was built and put into operation, and then closed by the congress of 1947. I lived in it when I was up at Lame Deer the late summer and fall of 1949. It was empty, while around 70 percent of the Cheyenne families had tuberculosis in their midst. The thin land is poorer, and everything costs more now. The little jobs the Indians used to pick up around the ranches and farms are almost gone in the slump in farm and stock prices. Your sister knows how little grass there is on their reservation; white ranchers tell me that there is just about enough grass to keep 10 white families (with the finances and know-how that white men would have). The Indians have only the know-how. Cheyennes are generally good ranchers. Their hope has always been the coal and oil on their reservation, but promoters and exploiters have always tried to get at these resources without having to meet the standard contracts that the federal government demands, the same contracts the white men would get easily. Now that the Indian Bill is turning the Indians over to the mercies of the states, there won't be that

I Do Not Apologize

problem and soon the Cheyennes will be starved into selling their resources for whatever is offered. There's a bill coming up now to do the same thing to the Menominees in Wisconsin.

This Indian Bill, railroaded through the last session of Congress, in its dying days, turns the Indians over to the states without any decision by the Indians. I'm enclosing copies of some of the editorials urging Eisenhower to veto this, but he signed it. There is no longer the federal legal staff, expert in Indian rights and treaties, or the government trusteeship to protect the natural resources of the Indians.

Most of the above has gone into a short piece the International News Service may carry for the Association on American Indian Affairs. I've written the piece at their request, but since it urges protection for the Indian's property and his rights, from exploiters and expropriators, it may not get put on the wires. At least we made an effort.

May 1954 be good to you, and to the Indians—
Sincerely, and in great haste,

————

MARCH 15, 1954

Mr. David Blackhoop, Chairman,
Standing Rock Sioux Tribal Council,
Fort Yates, North Dakota

Dear Mr. Blackhoop:
Enclosed is a carbon of a letter to Frank Productions about the moving picture of the life of Sitting Bull. You are very right to complain about the filming of the picture outside of this country, far from the Dakotas, when both region and background characters might so easily be authentic.

I am also interested in the protest of the South Dakota tribal councils, and yours, against Public Law 280. I hear the same complaint from Montana, Nebraska, and Oklahoma, and indirectly from many, many other Indians.

I trust that united action will help save the resources of the Indians.
Sincerely,

————

Association on American Indian Affairs

Dear Doctor Lesser:

The Mississippi Valley Historical Association [conference] was well attended until noon yesterday. Then Harry Truman cancelled his talk for last
night, as the enclosed clips show. I was told that the newspaper and radio
set-up of the meeting was concentrated on that talk and, of course, it all col-
lapsed, as most of the meeting did. There was almost no one around today.

The Indian talks yesterday were good of their kind, but kept well within
their announced topics and scopes. There was little beyond 1907 and that
only by implication—mostly a terse exposition of the Indian's concept of
private property, with no occasion for discussion on the present at all.

Many, noticing the "Association on American Indian Affairs" on my
badge, stopped to talk about Indians, particularly men from the Dakotas
and Oklahoma, but they were all teachers and the studies they had under
way were almost entirely of the historic period rather than the present.
Almost no one responded to queries about the present, nor had any interest
he was willing to put into words. I did give away the material I had with me,
all you sent me and the magazine, and so on, but I think the whole venture
was pretty much a loss. If I ever do this again, would it be possible to set up
a table and a chair or two, with a supply of material? Or is this against the
Association's policy? I've not given this any thought; it just occurred to me
when I saw how people clustered around anything that had something to
be picked up.

Sorry,

————

AUGUST 27, 1955

Mrs. Roy M. Green,
1845 South 41st Street
Lincoln 6, Nebraska.

Dear Norma:

For your Indian problem there is no stopping place between a half a
dozen clippings and a year's research and study. The publications by the
Association on American Indian Affairs are the best source around. They

dig out material on injustices, etc. Not that anything can be done about them under this current administration. Under Truman we at least managed to get the Commissioner fired. But Emmons, banker in the Navajo region and, I'm convinced, front for all the interests that are taking over all the Indian's natural resources, can't be pushed out of the Commissionership. I'm writing the AAIA to send you some literature if they can.

One of the best studies of one Indian group predicament is the one made of the Rapid City, South Dakota situation by, if I recall correctly, the Quakers. Your librarian should be able to locate a copy of this. The situation has been aggravated a hundred fold since then. People who complain about the Indian's burgeoning birthrate should read DeCastro's *Geography of Hunger*. Borderline starvation populations are all like that. So long as Indians were well fed meat eaters, children could be spaced out so that mothers were never encumbered by more than one child that had to be carried in case they had to flee. Three, four generations of near starvation cut down the energy and initiative too.

PINE RIDGE RESERVATION, SOUTH DAKOTA
Babies born at the hospital for the 12 months ending June 30 numbered 231 live births and 13 stillbirths. During this same time 4,066 acres of trust land were sold in Shannon County; 13,690 acres in Washabaugh County; and 14,125 acres in Bennett County, a total of 31,821 acres. This is at the rate of 87 acres per day. The requests for sale of land runs 3 to 4 times this acreage. (*Sheridan County Star*, July 15, 1954.)

This shows you what is happening.

———

SEPTEMBER 24, 1955

Mamie Meredith,[17]
Lincoln, Nebraska.

Dear Mamie:
I'm sorry I never got to do anything about your request to write a letter for the Indians last spring. I've written so many hundred of such letters for many years in an effort to get decent educational and health facilities for them, particularly education and training, to avoid the present shocking situation, but you can see how little it helped.

Under Eisenhower the replies to my letters from Senators and Representatives have too often been plain and very rude requests to keep to my own business. In the meantime the Indians are forced off the little land they had, cheated out of their grazing, mineral and timber rights, and the big interests and their tools in Congress have no intention of listening to anyone who would halt the expropriation. It's exactly like back in the Grant administration, except that perhaps the bullet and cannon ball was a little more merciful.

Norma Kidd Green plans to do a little something about the Lincoln situation. I sent her a handful of material. But it is really too late to do anything much now. The signs "No Indians Allowed" have gone up in public places all over the country.

This is an ungracious letter to send a fine generous person like you. But it's from one who has fought in these wars from back in the Hoover administration. All he did was to appoint a commission to investigate the matter, and to publish the horrifying finding in a thick blue volume neatly lettered in gold.[18]

Sincerely,

————

NOVEMBER 26, 1955

James D. King, Secretary,
Northern Cheyenne Tribal Council,
Lame Deer, Montana.

Dear James King:

It is fine to hear from you, and that you are secretary to the Tribal Council. They need someone like you to make contact with the outside world.

Yes, you should be able to buy overshoes for the Cheyenne children wholesale. I don't know where, but I am certain it could be managed. I suppose that there will be difficulty because there are storekeepers at Lame Deer and manufacturers will feel they must be protected and will probably refuse to sell to the council unless you set up your own store. Otherwise it would have to be through the personal interest of some manufacturer in the Cheyennes. I've tried to recall if there were any among the hundreds who wrote in about my book, but I can't recall one. I'll try to think of someone to write who might have friends among such manufacturers. I think many overshoes are now made in Missouri. You might look at the address on some in the stores at Lame Deer and write them. [. . .]

Would the county relief offices have names of wholesalers who would fill your orders? I wish you every success—we had no overshoes until I was about ten or eleven and had frozen my feet until the ends of all my toes festered off to the bone, nails and all. It's not something to wish on the small Cheyennes. [. . .]

Write me now and then how the people are getting along, and if there is anything in which I might be more helpful than I am in the shoes.

Best wishes for a fine warm holiday,

———

MARCH 3, 1956

Mrs. Myra K. Peters,[19]
Story, Wyoming.

Dear Myra Peters,

It's fine to hear from you and from Story in the Big Horns—almost my favorite mountains, and to have your very kind invitation.

I, too, am sad about the fight the Crows have on their hands,[20] but I've discovered that there is no use appealing to Washington under this administration. The only results have been insulting replies telling me I know nothing of the situation and to mind my own business. This has been the tone of reply from members of the executive branch and from the legislature, particularly those involved with interests wanting the Indian expropriated—men representing oil, coal, uranium and ranching.

Such interests have always been around, from 1620 on, but the rapid unlanding of such people as the Sioux within the last three years, and their gravitation to shacks and tents at the edges of towns as far away as Omaha and Chicago is appalling to me. With the shrinking ranch income they are driven to seek town employment, untrained, unfitted to cope with the discrimination they meet everywhere now, unable to get jobs. I saw some around Christmas-time in Omaha, Lincoln, Gordon and Scottsbluff.

I'll write to Washington about the Yellowtail dam, but I think it will be time wasted.

[. . .]

I'm sorry I can't take advantage of your fine invitation, but I'll be through the region some time next fall, and if I get up to Sheridan, I'll call you.

Thank you for the kind words about my books,

———

Mr. Deane DuComb
Box 5, Morganfield, Kentucky

Dear Mr. DuComb:

Ah, the sorghum's fine—a Kentucky family out home used to make it, but they always complained that the hot dry summers out there gave it a rough edge—I notice yours is particularly mellow, mellower it seems to me than the Kentucky product I've had the luck to taste before.

About the outgrown clothing of your girls: Indeed, there are Indians who can use all they can get. If you want to send these to the Cheyennes, I suggest Mrs. Margot Pringle Liberty, Birney Day School, Birney, Montana. This tiny village, of almost entirely one room log huts, is where the Sacred medicine Hat is kept, and is particularly poor, because so many of the families were remnants of the Little Wolf-Dull Knife flight north and so were given the last choice in land. The Keeper of the Hat, Limpy, is, I think, the son of the Limpy who was on that flight. Mrs. Liberty seems greatly interested in the Cheyennes, from the smallest to the oldest.

If you wish the Sioux to have the clothing, you might send it to Father Best, Gordon, Nebraska. He is a young Episcopalian Father, much interested in the displaced Indians who have been living in shacks and tents around Gordon, through 30 below zero winters, The superintendent, Pine Ridge Indian Agency, Pine Ridge, South Dakota, can tell you who would look after any distribution of clothing sent to the Sioux there. There have been recent changes to the administration there, and I don't know the new people.

From Mrs. Liberty I gather her pupils and the whole community are as ragged and hungry as ever, with the bad prices in meat and sugar beets, the little part time jobs that gave the Cheyennes an average of $45 to $75 cash income per year have just about vanished.

May the holidays at the DuComb's be particularly fine ones,

————

DECEMBER 22, 1956

Dear Father Powell,

It was fine to see you, and to know that you, at least, are willing to keep working for the Indians, no matter how hopeless it seems.

I was much interested in the enclosed version of your talk to the Chicago Westerners. You have gathered some very telling material and presented it with sincerity and convincing moderation—more moderation than I could have mustered, I am certain.

There is only one point that you may have under-stressed, and that is the part that House Resolution 1063 played in this, the start of all the current expropriation of Indians. The bill, as you know, made no provision for any [Indian] voice in the transfer of the tribes from the Indian Bureau to the states. Once more he was like the wooden Indian set on rollers, to be pushed wherever it suited the white man. As you also know, at the time of this quickie bill, shot through congress in the dying hours of the session, before either the Indians or their friends could hear of it, there was a real roar of protest from the press. This included pretty much all the press of the nation, from the *New York Herald-Tribune* and the *Times*, to such Indian country papers as the *Albuquerque New Mexico Journal*. Even the Hearst papers asked Eisenhower not to sign the bill. The Association on American Indian Affairs got out a sheet, "Press Comment on New Indian Law" at the time, but by then the bill was signed. I was at Wisconsin, deep in my novel class. I did not hear of the bill's being brought up until the last minute, and then it was signed. Not that I could have done anything—

But I am happy to see your strong arm added to the fight. And may its strength grow all the coming year, and years. May the sun shine warm upon all your household and all the charges that you see as yours.

Sincerely,

———

MARCH 16, 1957

Jeri Finley,[21]
Route 3, Box 376
Boise, Idaho.

Dear Jeri Finley:

I am very happy to know that you liked my *Crazy Horse* and *Cheyenne Autumn*. I am always particularly pleased to know that a westerner found these books worth reading.

You're right, I don't have much use for New York except as a base of operations, particularly to the Military and Indian Archives at Washington and various manuscript and obscure publications material on the Indian days in eastern repositories. But some years I spend only four or five months here. Next month, I get as far west as Wyoming.

Yes, the Sioux, like many other Indians, are in very unhappy circumstances. Without the training to fit well into white man towns they are being forced off the reservation into the surrounding towns, which have no way of assimilating them. I've tried to get some action on these things but with the cattlemen wanting their range, the Indians or the Indians' friends have little chance of being heard. Recently, however, it seems that the new Congressman from South Dakota, George McGovern, House of Representatives, Washington, D.C. is interested in initiating a full-scaled investigation into the current Indian question if he can scare up enough letters and so on to get some interest stirred up in Congress. You might think about dropping him a note.

In Gordon, Nebraska, Father Best and his Episcopalian group is working hard with the young Oglala Sioux that have been pushed off Pine Ridge into his town. This is, of course, on a non-sectarian level, as is Father Powell's work with the many young Indians that have found their way to Chicago, and are also untrained for life or a living there. There's an item in the Dec. 15, 1956 *Christian Science Monitor* about the problem of getting an education if you're an American Indian.

The Association on American Indian Affairs, 48 E. 88th Street, New York 28, N.Y. would send you an offset of this if you sent them a post card.

Anyway, I am happy to know that you are interested.

Sincerely,

———

MARCH 16, 1957

Mr. Leonard Jennewein,[22]
Dakota Wesleyan University,
Mitchell, South Dakota.

Dear Mr. Jennewein:

As you know the time has long been ripe for the "full scale, top-flight examination of the Indian problem" you thoughtfully suggest and I'm happy that you have crystallized it for the rest of us. I've shown your letter to Mrs. Emmie Mygatt here, who was flying out to Lame Deer, Montana, because of a very bad situation there among the Cheyennes. She writes books of fiction about them and the region and has become deeply involved. I am sure she will write Congressman McGovern. Her husband runs a tourist bureau here, and they have a summer home in the Big Horns. Republicans, they

I Do Not Apologize

were greatly disappointed with a trip to Washington to intercede with Emmons for the Cheyennes in the unlanding that is progressing so fast there too, land with coal and oil.

Have you been in touch with Father Peter John Powell, St. Timothy's Church, 3555 West Huron St., Chicago? He's deeply involved. He gave, as you may know, a talk to the Chicago Westerners that got an immediate protest from Washington to his bishop. A somewhat denatured version of this was published in the Chicago corral's magazine.

Your Congressman McGovern sounds like a valuable man and if I weren't so pressed by deadlines and speaking dates, I should have been to Washington to see him before now. Unfortunately I can't make it before I go west as far as Laramie to give some talks scheduled long ago.

More power to you,

————

APRIL 6, 1957

Mr. F. H. Sinclair,[23]
Sheridan Press Building
Sheridan, Wyoming.

Dear Neckyoke Jones:
Yes, I hear sad tales from the Tongue River, as I hear sad tales from all the Indians from the Plains. Nor is it any better elsewhere, it seems. I discovered in Wisconsin that, by putting the Menominees under the state, the lumber hogs got at the last piece of big timber left in the state. By good management these Indians had been able to preserve their timber, and have a steady income. Last summer I saw only stumps and toppings, everything stripped where even a year ago trees really grew to touch the sky. The extermination policy of the Grant administration was nothing compared to what we have now.

I should hate to see the Medicine Hat carted off by some dry-tongued young Cheyenne, but I am convinced that if the Hat leaves the Cheyennes in any way whatsoever, the People will really go to pieces. It was predicted long, long ago that if the Hat falls into alien hands, the Northern Cheyennes will vanish from the earth, and I wouldn't be one to involve myself in getting the Hat into white man hands. Only if there were a Cheyenne shrine set up on the Custer Hill, under the auspices of the Cheyennes, could I approve such a move. What there should be is an Indian Memorial Museum in the

Plains Indian country, with a board of all the tribes, and then there could be a place for such items. In such a project I should be happy to help.

Sincerely,

————

MAY 25, 1957

Representative George McGovern,
House of Representatives,
Washington, D.C.

Dear Mr. McGovern:
Just before I headed out west to Nebraska and Wyoming for some research and some speaking, the latter largely about Indians, I received a letter from your field representative, Leonard Jennewein, about your deep interest in the American Indian and the possibilities of a full scale, top-flight examination of the whole Indian question. I mentioned this with my approval here and there on my trip and I hope you received some letters. At Nebraska I said a little about the current plight of the Indians to the Phi Beta Kappa–Sigma Xi dinner, very little really, but enough to cause Mrs. Abel, former senator from Nebraska, to gather up her guests and walk out on me.

I have been hoping that a trip to Washington would come up so I could take advantage of Mr. Jennewein's invitation to drop in at your office to hear something of your plans, but I haven't been able to manage it. I am very sorry.

Have you had any success with your plans for the contemplated investigation? I am deep in a book on cattle on the Great Plains, and far behind my deadline, but if there is anything I can do to help your efforts for the Indians I should be happy.

Sincerely,

————

APRIL 16, 1958

Dear LaVerne Madigan:[24]
Enclosed are a couple of clippings about the "We Shake Hands" program. I trust the weather wasn't too cold out on Pine Ridge. It got pretty bad since you were out—

I Do Not Apologize

I got in a couple of licks for the Indians in my interview on Martha Deane's program this morning. She brought up Clark's article on the "Indian Raid of the Treasury" in the *Reader's Digest* for March, and I gave what I could about the way the Black Hills were bought—under pressure of guns and starvation, with the chiefs locked in the stockade at Red Cloud until they signed. I also got in a bit on the present situation of the Indians. It was too brief to give a sound idea, but I've had calls all afternoon and evening about the things I said.

Keep up the good work—I'm off to Nebraska for some research and autographing.

Sincerely,

———

NOVEMBER 2, 1958

Winona A. Cromwell,[25]
Coyote Pass,
Hemet, California.

Dear Winona Cromwell:

Thank you. It is fine to know that someone so closely associated with the Oglala Sioux finds *Crazy Horse* a book to "treasure."

You are very right. Crucial times in the lives of a people do seem to produce great men. Perhaps, like diamonds, they are crystallized by the heat of stress and pressure. And it is true, I think, as you suggest, that the earth never forgets the blood spilled upon her.

Unfortunately, our spilling of Indian blood is not yet over. True, we no longer shoot the women and children down, but—thrust into beggary, thievery and prostitution around the fringes of our cities, to which they were driven, without a way to make a decent livelihood—isn't that an even more cruel kind of bloodshed?

"We cannot even die in honor now," a Cheyenne woman told me sadly down in Omaha. She and her husband had been lured from the reservation on the guarantee of a job at Omaha, only to find it was one with no expectation at all that the untrained Indian could hold. But, once off the reservation, his little plot of land sold for money to move to Omaha—there was nowhere to go, and no jobs.

But enough—Thank you very much for writing.

———

JANUARY 22, 1960

John Woodenlegs, President,
Northern Cheyenne Tribe,
Lame Deer Montana

Dear Mr. Woodenlegs:

In the Association on American Indian Affairs *News Letter*, I read of the Northern Cheyenne "Fifty Years Unallotment Program" to save your homes and your lands.

Because the Northern Cheyennes are very dear to my heart, I had 50 copies of this run off and sent to people who wrote me friendly letters about my two Cheyenne books, *Cheyenne Autumn* and *The Horsecatcher*, with the request that they write the Indian Bureau, urging that you be given every aid and encouragement in this project. Your plan seems to be an excellent one to utilize some of the genius of the Cheyennes as a people and I wish you every success.

Cheyenne Autumn will never sell enough copies to pay for my actual expenses in the long research and all the travel and time in Washington, D.C. in the archives. It's apparently full of the truth that makes the white man feel ashamed, or so it seems. *The Horsecatcher*, however, has paid for my expenses and so I am sending you part of the recent royalties to be used for some particularly urgent purpose for the betterment of the people.

May 1960 be the opening of a fine new decade for the Cheyennes everywhere.

Sincerely,

———

JANUARY 30, 1960

F. H Sinclair

Dear Neckyoke;

Just a hasty note in the midst of proofreading, etc.

As you may know, I've been sending and having others send great boxes of clothing, etc., from here and from Nebraska to the Cheyennes for many years. But these things are, really, shameful, for they are mean little half measures. What I am interested in, as I was when I went on "Strike It Rich" many years ago for the Cheyenne artists in the Tongue River schools, is the

I Do Not Apologize

opportunity they should have to make something of their magnificent heritage as artists and as human beings who need not be beholden to any of us.

I see what the unlanding of the Indians has done the last few years from the city end of it. I see it at Scott's Bluff, where they are at least treated more like human beings than most places. I see it in the shack town at Lincoln, at Omaha, at Rapid City, at Chicago and I see it here. It is a sinful and shameful thing—this driving the Indians by psychological pressures into a life for which we have given them absolutely no fitness, no way of making a living or even an existence. I think it is time we tried to make it possible for the Indians to get something of an education and to make something of the pitiful bits of land left to them. I saw it on the Cheyenne reservation when I was up there; I saw it last summer at Pine Ridge. I think we are operating under an Extermination Policy every bit as damnable as the butchery under Grant and Sheridan and the men who initiated it long before them. I'm sick of Indian do-gooders who work so hard to help those who would take the last bit of property from him.

Sincerely,

———

FEBRUARY 18, 1960

Fred A. Seaton, Secretary of the Interior,
Washington, D.C.

Dear Mr. Secretary:

You are a very busy man, with large projects demanding your attention every minute, but I should like to beg a bit of time for a most unfortunate people, the Northern Cheyennes up at Lame Deer, Montana.

As a Nebraskan you know something of the story of the Northern Cheyennes, their attempts to remain peaceful through the 1850–1877 period with repeated failure to receive the goods and annuities due them under the treaties of 1851, 1868, and 1876, their unlucky availability as peaceful bands when Indians, any Indians, had to be "punished" for depredations—the guilty anticipating military action and safely far away. You'll know of the desperate flight north from Indian Territory in 1878 and the decimation of Dull Knife's band on the winter snows around Fort Robinson.

Perhaps you have been up on the Northern Cheyenne Reservation on the Tongue River and know how broken the land is, how poor for any possible existence on small plots. Good, however, as tribal lands, with tribal herds as their current "Fifty Year Unallotment Program" anticipates, the Cheyennes have an excellent chance to succeed as apparently your Department has decided, enough at least to arouse expressions of encouragement from your Assistant Secretary, Roger S. Ernst.

The Cheyennes are good cattlemen; had a fine herd, the debt on it paid off when the winter of 1949 cleaned them out, as it did many of the white ranchers. But most of the white men had financial backlogs and credit to go on. The Indians, in their poverty, on fragmented acreage, surrounded by general covetousness, had neither.

I know what the situation was then; I lived on the reservation for some time in that bad year of 1949, finishing up research for my *Cheyenne Autumn*. In an effort to help the Indians if I could, I took their plight to the Bureau of Indian Affairs, even to the President. The real obstacle, I found then, and as it seems to be now, was right there in Montana: the people on and off the Reservation who wanted the range, the oil, the coal. I went up to the area office at Billings, in September of 1949 and was met with less than common courtesy by a couple of the key men in charge.

From the Indians, and others interested in their welfare, I gather that the situation has not changed. Some local interests and the area office are still the real obstacles to any chance for self sufficiency for the Cheyennes on their reservation.

May I ask that you have this matter given a bit of thought by someone in your office, please? You know that I would not ask this of you if I did not think that in good conscience neither you or I can refuse to do all we can to give these people one last chance.

Sincerely,

———

CIRCA JUNE 2, 1960

Helen Hector
Editorial Offices,
The Reader's Digest
Pleasantville, NY

Dear Helen Hector:

I am sorry that my article on the Sioux took up so much of your time. Your criticism is, of course, just. Unfortunately any article about the Sioux "from the angle of religion, art of living, death" as your letter of May 24 suggested might well have the flaws you found.

The real difficulty, however, was the vast difference in the Sioux situation since 1952 when you published the earlier article. Almost any example or anecdote to illustrate the good of Sioux life has become unsuited to a periodical of wide circulation because it would suggest a real criticism of the present administration which, the Indians say, "has taken away everything we had left and given us only alcohol to drown our misery."

During the dying days of the Congress of 1953 HR 1063, turning the Indians over to the states without any consent of the Indians, was passed. Every newspaper of any consequence asked President Eisenhower to veto it. It was signed and the reservations opened to all kinds of exploitation. Much of the land was sold at public auction for practically nothing, because the Indians had no money and so the price was kept down by the same old white man collusion that kept the lease money down. Thousands and thousands of the Sioux were forced off the reservations, driven to the small towns around the reservations where no work was even available, or as far off as Chicago, without the education, the training, or other preparation for making a living in any town except by theft, or prostitution.

I saw the same thing happen to the Menominees in Wisconsin. They had the only big trees left in the state, managed under federal trusteeship. This gave the small tribe a good and perpetual livelihood from the careful harvesting of lumber, to which they added considerably from tourists and the hunting and fishing of the lovely region. After the 1953 bill they were left only cutover stump land—all the perpetual income gone in one season. I saw this happen—beautiful magnificent trees carefully harvested one summer, the next only stumps and toppings, with a lone porcupine loping sadly along the unused road looking for a tree big enough to climb.

Practically any example of the good life I might have given you could have been directly challenged by the realities of the new degradation. True, the last two years the pressure has been eased on the Northern Cheyennes in Montana through direct appeals to the Secretary of the Interior, Fred Seaton and others, assisted considerably, I have been told, by the wide distribution of my little novel of a Cheyenne boy, *The Horsecatcher*, published in *Reader's Digest Condensed Books*.

The Sioux situation is still so tragic I could weep if those Indians hadn't taught me not to cry. I am sorry I couldn't get a little sympathy for them through the article.

Sincerely,

MS:c

Enclosed: Copy of some editorials against HR 1063.

———

JUNE 5, 1961

Charles Barrett[26]
Long Island, Maine

Dear Charles Barrett:

You are a patient man. I'm sorry I am so negligent about answering letters. The writing has to come first—

But there are the Indians. Perhaps I wrote you of my uneasiness about the talk the Assistant Secretary for the Interior gave at the meeting of the Association on American Indian Affairs, particularly when he said he wanted to make it clear that the Bureau of Indian Affairs wasn't for Indians. I wanted to ask why not, when the Department of commerce was for commerce, the Department of Agriculture for the farmer. Then I remember that farmers in Omaha once rotten-egged Secretary Benson.

Well, take it easy—and take a look at the sunny sky for me.

Sincerely,

————

P.S. I'm adding a copy of the "White Cross American Indian Foundation" of the Leighs. As I noted on the copy, I don't know these people but I know the Sioux of Pine Ridge were desperate last winter. Big Joe Rosenfield of the Big Joe program, WABC, sent something like $400.00 up to Wounded Knee for a community well which, I'm told was dug and desperately welcome.

OCTOBER 15, 1961

Sam J. Ervin, Jr. Chairman,
Senate Judiciary Subcommittee on Constitutional Rights,
United States Senate, Washington, D.C.

Dear Senator Ervin:

Although I am not an Indian I appreciate the "Questionnaire to Individual Indians" that you sent to me. I grew up around the Sioux friends of my father, Jules Sandoz, and as an adult I made a close study of the Plains Indians from prehistoric times. I have spent considerable time on both the Pine Ridge and the Tongue River Reservations. I published various magazine articles on the Plains Indians and four books: *Crazy Horse*, 1942; *Cheyenne Autumn*, 1953; *The Horsecatcher*, 1957, and *These Were the Sioux*, 1961.

With this background I feel qualified to say that a serious study of the constitutional rights of the American Indian is long overdue. [. . .] There are, it seems to me some pertinent considerations beyond the strict legal interpretations of constitutional rights. For example, what is the proper constitutional protection for the Indians whose ancestors were:

1. Pursued by troops on the Indian's treaty-right territory until practically every man and boy of courage, intelligence, and initiative died trying to protect the women and children from the soldier bullets.

2. Cheated out of their lands by treaties not kept or treaties thrust upon them by gun, stockade and cannon.

3. Herded to shrinking reservations so poor no white man of the moment wanted the land. Often unaccustomed to agriculture, they were to dig a living from the reluctant earth, the treaty provided rations that were issued sustaining them barely above starvation levels, so the Indians of today are the product of four, five generations of malnutrition.

4. Deprived of their religion, one which had fitted their environment, temperament, and upon which their whole social, ethical, and philosophical concept of good life depended. Not only the ceremonials and the dances were forbidden but even the songs, despite the constitutional guarantees of religious freedom.

5. Deprived of the treaty promised schooling, with the only real opportunity offered the penniless Indian youth for an education, Carlisle, closed in the face of the grandfathers. How many white children from illiterate, bookless homes, and from the poor reservation schools could hope to meet the requirements for college scholarships? How many young Indians are discouraged or actually shut out of the reservation high schools by the overcrowding? How many have no real opportunity for even a poor rural school education? Draft boards are finding young men from reservations who never went to school long enough to speak passable English, much less read and write it.

Decimated, starved, robbed of substance, of culture and religion, deprived of both pride and dignity, both the ancestors and the Indians of today sought to escape from the stark reality in any way possible, whether in the Ghost Dancing of the 1889–90 period or the alcoholism of today. In many regions this situation was aggravated by the passage of H.R. 1063 in 1953. Often the Indians are victimized by practically any white man or group offering a whiskey bottle or something to tide the hungry family through the next winter in exchange for the earth, coal, oil, or other permanent wealth that had escaped the sharp eyes of the early reservation planners.

Without land and driven from the poor reservations by the thousands since 1953, too often without any training or preparation for existence in a modern town or city, the Indians today are frequently condemned to life in desperate privation, some squalid tenement or in a tar-paper shack, or tent colony at the fringes of some embarrassed city. With no employment open, and return to the reservation closed behind him, his land gone to a one-bid auction, often the only living that the Indian or his wife and daughter can eke out is by theft or prostitution, both offenses that once brought ostracism by many tribes.

What, I wonder, could one call the constitutional rights of such a man, a man of such condition in the United States of America today? It is true that the Indian needs to have his constitutional rights protected, but even more urgent is the rebuilding of his nutrition starved body, his hope starved mind. He needs training for living in white society, and the opportunity to use his intelligence, initiative, ingenuity, and imagination that are his native heritage. Give him these weapons and the Indian will fight those who would deprive him of his constitutional rights as he fought Custer on the ridge of the Little Big Horn.

Sincerely,

————

JANUARY 28, 1963

Secretary Stewart L. Udall
Department of the Interior
Washington, D.C.

Dear Secretary Udall:
RE: The Crazy Horse Monument, Black Hills, South Dakota:[27]
It is a phenomenal piece of luck for all of us that Korczak Ziolkowski, the sculptor from Boston, should have caught the vision of a great monument to the American Indian rooted in the heart of the continent. It is fitting that the monument should portray Crazy Horse, the man who embodied in a tremendous measure the innate greatness of all his race—the pride, dignity, and vision—to stand out from a mountain of living granite that will outlast the ages.

It is fine to know that you are interested in this vast undertaking. Anything that you can do to assist in its completion will receive a long gratitude.

With work on the mountain moving ahead as it should, Mr. Ziolkowski's plans for an Indian Cultural Center will receive a tremendous impetus. That, too, is important for the preservation and perpetuation of the crafts, the arts, and the history of the American Indian, and to nurture the genius of this people into the future.

Sincerely,

———

SEPTEMBER 26, 1964

Eleanor Phelps[28]
New York 21, N.Y.

Dear Eleanor Phelps:

Please forgive this delay in my reply to your fine letter about the Indians and *Cheyenne Autumn*. Thank you.

Yes, whenever anyone charged the government with complete dishonesty toward the Indians, there was always the Seneca treaty to which the apologists could point. Now that too is broken.[29] The Indians were treated with peculiar cynicism during the Eisenhower administration, stripped of the last of any possessions worth having, leaving, as the Indians wrote me, not even the dignity of dying fighting, as they could in the old days.

It is true there's little one person can do, but together we have power. There is a fairly serious effort made now, a hundred, in many cases two hundred years late, to open real education and training for life as it must be lived. An exceptional young person of any other color could get as much education as he could absorb, even though he was penniless, but not the Indians, not after Carlisle was closed, before 1910.

Work through your federal representatives. Hound them about the treatment of the Indians. Some find working with the Association on American Indian Affairs helpful. They can at least help keep you informed where the latest steal is taking place.

I keep a list of the current committees of Congress "entrusted" with Indian affairs and I deluge them with letters if I'm not digging away at some archives and not aware of what's going on. But someone has to make the world a little more aware of the dignity and philosophical worth of the Indian ways that we destroyed.

Sincerely,

JANUARY 30, 1965

Mrs. Mary Zeisler
Brooklyn, New York 11203

Dear Mrs. Zeisler:

[...]

You are perfectly right. If each one of us "sits back in his chair and waits for someone else" to do something about the continued injustices to the American Indians, nothing will be done, and yet if one could get the good will of the nation organized now, even during the last few years against the constant draining away of the last treaty guaranteed possessions of the Indian, such a tribe as the Senecas would not be flooded from their traditional home lands, guaranteed forever by the signature of even George Washington, or the water rights of some western tribes, the hunting and fishing of the Alaskan peoples, the range, coal, oil, uranium, etc. of tribes scattered everywhere.

And this on top of the extermination policy of the early white man's government from the Atlantic seaboard to the Pacific, and back only a few miles from where I later grew up—the massacre of Wounded Knee, South Dakota in 1890. [...]

I am enclosing an *Indian Affairs Newsletter* of the Association of American Indian Affairs, 432 Park Avenue, New York City. These people try to expose some of the trickery and arouse us to action. Even an occasional postcard to your congressman can help, if there are others working too. There is material available free from the Bureau of Indian Affairs, Department of Interior, Washington, D.C. giving the "official" point of view, and some of the things that are planned or in progress. A word there too can help stop the mischievous, promote the good.

Sincerely,

JULY 19, 1965

Norma Kidd Green
Edgewood on Long Lake
Park Rapids, Minnesota

Dear NKG:

I'm just recovering from a relapse and a summer cold, but I'll take a moment about the matter of the Omaha Self-Government Plan.

Most Indian tribes had such a plan going the rounds after the real disillusionment with the agency system. Often it was the product of those in no way connected with the agency "hangers-on," but none of the plans got anywhere.

I recall when Coin Harvey was up in the late 1920s, talking to Dr. Sheldon in the basement of Old U Hall. I was copying Red Cloud material for Sheldon and was called from the back to bring my portable to the table out at the front to take down the outline of Coin's idea of the Inca system of government directly on the typewriter as I often did. The talk drifted through various Indian governmental systems, and the later movements on the Reservations. Dr. Sheldon mentioned the Oglala pattern that was formed by the anti-Red Cloud faction, and spoke of the self-government systems worked out by the Otoes and the Omahas on the reservations, with apparently more progress among the latter because there was more discontent there. However, I don't recall the outlines of either now. I do remember that Harvey considered them both "rudimentary" compared to the Inca system. He was a little touched on that subject by then, or so I thought at the time.

That's all I remember about the notes I took for Harvey.

Sorry,

———

OCTOBER 18, 1965

Mildred Holmes
19 Middle Street
Eastport, Maine 04631

Dear Mildred Holmes:

[...]

Your interest in the Passamaquoddy Indians is a fine one. Eastern Indians were neglected far too long before any really open-minded approaches to them as anything but blood-thirsty enemies seem to have been attempted. About the origins of these people, have you tried the index volume of the Bureau of Ethnology Reports? That might be a good start. Perhaps the Maine Library Commission sends books around, books not readily available in your libraries.

Most of the warring, after the whites pushed in, forced the Indians westward. So the Sioux came to the Plains along with two Algonquin tribes, the Cheyennes and Arapahos.

I haven't noticed that the Indian has profited any from the Negro gain in civil rights. The Indian is not a noisy pusher. I wish he were. As it stands, the Indians still have the problem of a decent education and training for life in the modern world.

Among the Cheyennes there have been more applicants for high school work than can be accommodated—a situation that is of long, long standing. It was true in Hoover's administration and was little improved except for a short time under Roosevelt. Now the situation is to be remedied, but by the states, and I am dubious of state intervention so long as the Indians have a bit of property that the white ranchers, oil men, coal men, and other mining interests want. I saw Wisconsin destroy the great trees of the Menominees after the state took their reservation over, the last great trees left in Wisconsin, and with them the livelihood of the Indians as lumbermen, resort owners, hunting guides, and so on. All they have left is cutover lands, with a few tardy attempts to replenish the great pines on the scheme that the federal government had started. And, if Wisconsin is without conscience, what state can one trust?

Children from isolated, illiterate homes need a strong push by "head start" and more if they are to make anything of themselves. And after the start there must be something besides escape into the whiskey bottle of the whites who want the little property the Indians retain.

Sorry,

———

I Do Not Apologize

3.

Campaign

against

American

Indian

Stereotypes

I n addition to her letters of protest concerning federal Indian policies, Sandoz actively campaigned against the harmful negative
stereotypes of American Indian people that demonized them as
"godless savages." During these years in practically all popular media, especially film, American Indians were characterized as murderous, bloodthirsty
miscreants; drunkards devoid of culture; or as noble, yet doomed relics of
the past. These images ingrained skewed concepts about Native Americans
into non-Native minds and imaginations. The only "good" Indians were the
ones who stood firmly by the side of the white man offering help, friendship,
and protection from other "savages." Sandoz would have wholeheartedly
agreed with Choctaw scholar Devon Mihesuah that "no other ethnic group
in the United States has greater and more varied distortions of its cultural
identity than American Indians."[1] One of the most popular and widely ac-
claimed films of the era was John Ford's now classic film *The Searchers* (1956).
Starring John Wayne and Natalie Wood, this film presents American Indians (Comanches in this case) as murderous kidnappers who target, pillage,
and rape young white girls. Choctaw film studies scholar Jacquelyn Kilpatrick writes that in this particular film, "blatant racist ideas abound. . . . No
in depth attempt to humanize the Comanches is made."[2] And while most
Americans eschew these negative images and stereotypes today, it is important to remember that Sandoz was writing against them in the early 1940s.
These stereotypes irked her significantly, and those of Indian women particularly. In a 1945 letter to her friend Ed Fitzgerald, who had written to ask
about "Indian Princesses," Sandoz remarks curtly that "the term 'Indian Princess' is a fancy of third rate poetry and the show business."[3]

Sandoz's books, *Crazy Horse: Strange Man of the Oglalas* and *Cheyenne Autumn* were both used as foundations for films. *Chief Crazy Horse*, directed by George Sherman and starring Victor Mature and Suzan Ball, debuted in 1955. Sandoz knew that much of the film was based on information that came directly from her book, and she believed she was plagiarized. However, what bothered her more was that such a mishmash of historical images and ideas could be produced.[4] John Ford's production of *Cheyenne Autumn*, which was expressly based on her book, riled her so that she briefly considered litigation, but decided against it, though she certainly thought the Native American descendants of the characters portrayed in the movie should sue for the shameless libels contained therein. Sandoz saw it as a clear case of "character assassination."[5]

In recent years, entire scholarly works have been devoted to addressing the negative impact of stereotypes on people of color, especially Native Americans. However, in the 1940s, '50s, and '60s, little or no "legitimate" research (read "white") had been done regarding such issues, especially about American Indians, and few spoke out against them. In fact, speaking out against films like these, especially during the dark years of the McCarthy-era 1950s, could easily have been construed as "un-American." Yet American Indians themselves had long been speaking out about the negative images as insidious, disheartening, and destructive to the well-being of their peoples. Native intellectuals such as Paiute teacher and writer Sarah Winnemucca Hopkins, Dakota physician and writer Charles Eastman, Lakota teacher and writer Luther Standing Bear, Osage scholar and writer John Joseph Matthews, and Cherokee activist and National Committee of American Indians executive secretary Ruth Muskrat Bronson wrote entire books in efforts to dispel commonly held stereotypes of Native Americans, but very few people paid attention. Film critics and writers Ralph and Natasha Friar were among the first white writers to indict Hollywood as "co-conspirators in committing cultural genocide by subverting the Native American's various ethnic identities and retaining him as a racial scapegoat," but this book did not appear until 1972.[6]

Granted, there were films and books produced during these years that presented sympathetic images of Native Americans. Images of the "child of nature" or "noble red man," while more well-intentioned, were nevertheless still bound in stereotype, relegating American Indians to dimensionless characters—still savages, but more agreeable. One such movie is *Broken Arrow*, directed by Delmer Daves and starring Jimmy Stewart, Jeff Chandler (Cochise), and Native actor Jay Silverheels (Geronimo). Based on the book

Mari Sandoz in her apartment, standing next to a portrait of herself. Note the boxes of letters atop the piano to the upper right. Caroline Sandoz Pifer Collection, Mari Sandoz High Plains Heritage Center—Chadron College. 2003.001.00138.

Blood Brother by Elliot Arnold, *Broken Arrow* tells a story of friendship between Chiricahua Apache leader, Cochise, and white scout/friend of the Indian, Tom Jeffords. In the movie, a Golden Globe winner, the main focus remains solidly on Jeffords as a man who understands Indians, while Cochise is presented as a noble, admirable Indian patriot who befriends Jeffords. Cochise, as a "good" Indian, stands with Jeffords against the "renegade," wild, violent, and resistant Apache leader, Geronimo.[7] There is a vast supply of Apache violence to go around. Cochise kills one of his own tribesmen who threatens Jeffords's life long after the danger has passed, and Cochise shows no remorse or even concern about killing a brother Apache. In balance, however, the viewer is also aware that the white men are violent, vindictive, and deceitful in their own ways. This movie was one of the earliest attempts to portray Native people as human beings whose motivations could be understood, and Sandoz endorsed the film through her connections with the Association on American Indian Affairs.

Television helped perpetuate Native American stereotypes as well—both negative and sympathetic images. Westerns were very popular; programming such as *Death Valley Days, Wagon Train,* and *Bonanza* were regular family fare, and often featured American Indians as "evil savages" or "noble red men," though these friendly Indians were usually just singular males. Native women were stereotyped in their own particular dichotomy—the "squaw/drudge" or the "Indian Princess"—images that set Sandoz's teeth on edge and ones she often castigated in her letters and wrote against in her books. She understood that the negative stereotypes white audiences, especially children, consumed about Native American people ultimately made their dispossession, colonization, and forced assimilation acceptable. She also hints in some of her letters that by continually presenting negative images and stereotypes of Native Americans, the popular media could easily squelch any feeling of positive self-esteem held by American Indians—who did (and do) read books and see films made during these decades. Several notable Native scholars and writers from various tribal backgrounds have addressed this issue in recent years, including Vine Deloria, Jr. (Dakota), Phillip Deloria (Dakota), Louis Owens (Choctaw/Cherokee), and Gieogamah Hanay (Kiowa/Delaware). Owens writes of seeing these images as a boy:

In nearly all the films I saw in theaters or on television, the Indians' role was to ride wildly in circles on painted ponies while sturdy white men crouched behind covered wagons and shot the Indians off their horses, one by one, to protect white women and children. . . . There was an ever present sense in these films that the Indian didn't count and was just a colorful residue of the past . . .[8]

Owens grew up to write back against such stereotypes as an adult, but how many other Native youth may have absorbed these images and believed the distortions? Although negative Native stereotypes arguably reached their zenith by the 1960s in film, the images linger on in various and costly ways. For example, both professional and college level sports are rife with entrenched Native American mascots, misrepresenting and exploiting the people in a most reprehensible manner. Sandoz never addressed the mascot issue, but she did criticize American cinema. She realized early on how damaging these unsavory images could be, and she never hesitated to address this issue and other historical inaccuracies in her missives to Hollywood notables.

I Do Not Apologize

But Hollywood wasn't the only venue to receive criticism from Sandoz. She felt strongly enough about this issue to enlighten other individuals through her letters. Part-and-parcel of her determination to set this record straight about American Indian stereotypes stems from her desire for historical accuracy; but embedded within that desire, I would argue, is her feeling that Native people needed to be portrayed as vital human beings deserving of dignity and consideration. For example, in a letter to Father George, a priest at St. Joseph's Indian School who had written Sandoz for a donation to his school, she can't help but question his choice of photographic presentation:

I have just one little question—why does everyone put those unSiouan head bands on the girls? These are so reminiscent of the patronizing, sentimental period that cost the Sioux so much in opportunity and self-respect. . . . I like to see the Sioux girls with the beaded bands hanging from the top of their braids. These meant so much, were so commonly recognized as the mark of a thoughtful, dutiful, and faithful Sioux maiden and young woman.[9]

Sandoz clearly finds these false representations distasteful, despite the fact that she does admire St. Joseph's Indian School for educating youngsters. Rather than send money to the church sponsored organization, Sandoz sent a book to the school. St. Joseph's is still operational, and still sending out pledge brochures featuring young Native American children striving for education and a "better life."

Despite her campaign against negative stereotyping, Sandoz at times was given to a certain amount of stereotyping of her own. She sometimes over-emphasized Indians as victims of devastating circumstances. It seems apparent that in an effort to gain a sympathetic audience, Sandoz crossed the line into sentimentalism and romanticism. Certainly, she knew the main audience for her books was composed of white people who had preconceived notions about Indians, and she sometimes drew on those very notions to drive home her point. In her letters to various representatives and senators, again most of whom were white, she called up the historical images of Lakotas and Cheyennes as "the greatest" warriors of the Plains, "their women among the finest quill and bead workers."[10] Still, she balances the images with those of Indians as survivors, employing the more romantic images to gain sympathy for their current situation. Or, perhaps in her eagerness to erase the negative stereotypes of Native Americans, Sandoz overbalances and in certain instances leaves the ideas of the "tragically doomed" Indians on the page. For example, in *Hostiles and Friendlies*, Sandoz describes the thoughts of the remaining Lakota leaders after Crazy Horse's death:

Who could say what further treachery the whites had planned for those of them who were left behind, men like Little Hawk, . . . Big Road, and He Dog and a dozen others? They could only expect death or imprisonment and perhaps as much for their families now that the only man who could stand up for them was dead.[11]

But even in this, Sandoz lays the blame for these unfortunate circumstances squarely at the feet of the whites. There is no mystery as to why the tragedy is happening. In her letters as well, Sandoz is clear in her assessment of the government's heavy hand as the major cause of the so-called "Indian Problem."

Additionally, Sandoz was undoubtedly influenced by her friend and colleague, Nebraskan author John G. Neihardt's sentimental view of American Indians as well. *Black Elk Speaks*, his most well-known publication, was a "perennial favorite," according to Stauffer.[12] Sandoz praised the book unstintingly, and promoted reprinting with the University of Nebraska Press's Bison Book endeavor in the early 1960s. Though it had been originally published in 1932, *Black Elk Speaks* only reached its target audience after the reprint of the 1960s, when interest exploded in Native American culture and philosophy. Though Neihardt and Sandoz corresponded only infrequently, the two remained friends and admirers of one another's work. Sandoz viewed herself more as a historian than did Neihardt, whose first love was the epic poem. And though Sandoz did not cite Neihardt's work in *Crazy Horse*, it seems clear that bits and pieces of information, similar imagery and phrasings, are shared in both books. However, I suspect that in some measure, Sandoz's repeated readings of Neihardt's work imbued her subconscious—including the romantic sentimentalism.

In the letters presented here, however, one finds that when Sandoz calls up romantic images of Native Americans, she has specific rhetorical reasons for doing so. For instance, in her letter to Massachusetts industrialist John S. Du Mont, we see an interesting mix of subtlety and salience in the use of romantic images of the past. Du Mont and a colleague, New York attorney John Parsons, were interested in going to the Northern Cheyenne Reservation to interview elders about the weaponry used in the Battle of the Little Big Horn. Sandoz agreed to write a letter of introduction for them to friend and tribal chairman Rufus Wallowing in 1953. After the visit to the reservation, Du Mont wrote to Sandoz complaining that Wallowing and Cheyenne tribal members had asked for monetary compensation for their time during the interviews, which stunned and dismayed both Du Mont and Parsons. In her response to Du Mont's lament that the Cheyennes were not eager to

I Do Not Apologize

share their information with strange white men for free, Sandoz begins by calling up the historical connections between the Cheyennes the men have just visited and those "heroic" Cheyennes of the past. Her words are intended to remind him that they are relatives of one another—ancestors. On the one hand, Du Mont and his friend admired, even idolized, the Cheyenne warriors who had fought Custer; but they were now castigating their descendants. Sandoz brings this to Du Mont's attention in a rather delicate manner. She avoids chiding him too much, for Du Mont is a powerful man of means who could use his position and money to help the Cheyennes; however, she is not going to let him off the hook easily either. While at one point she seems to agree with him, saying, "you're right about [Wallowing], he knows how to feather his nest," Sandoz is quick to qualify the statement by adding "as does every politician, white or red." Still later she reiterates the position of Wallowing as tribal chair, and says, "these characteristics . . . grow particularly strong in a captive people"[13]—a pointed reminder that the Northern Cheyennes are doing what they must to survive, and that they are indeed captives in the dominant white society in which Du Mont and Parsons have succeeded so well. Returning to the historical Cheyenne images that Du Mont so admires, Sandoz brings the letter full circle, and compares that image with the abhorrent conditions of the present-day reservation. The implications are clear: Du Mont and his friend should be ashamed for complaining about giving a few dollars to the hungry Cheyenne people in exchange for the information the two recreational historians wanted so desperately.

Sandoz was adamant in her campaign against negative stereotypes and images of Native Americans. That the American public could believe such propaganda about an entire group of people and promote such misinformation disheartened and disturbed her. As a responsible ally to Native peoples, Sandoz took every opportunity to set the record straight on this issue with all the fervor that she sought to promote historical accuracy in other venues, including research and politics. She understood as few others did during these years that as long as the negative images and stereotypes of American Indians were tolerated, absorbed, or promoted, mainstream Americans would have little sympathy for the serious situations that most Native American people were facing. The letters in this section are few in number, but important because they are filled with Sandoz's sharp insights to the questions of Native American stereotypes.

Ed Fitzgerald

Dear Fitzg's, Honeys:

About the lady Indian chiefs and princesses: There have been many women chiefs, usually through some special qualification or because the great men of their families had been killed, as in the case of Sitting Bull's Sioux, when they were brought back from Canada. Many bands had women heads then because the long years of fighting had been very costly. When their young men grew up to leadership years the women took their rightful places, as matriarchs in a matriarchal society. I knew several of these women when I was a girl, but with the customary modesty of people who have achieved greatness through travail, so it was not until I went into a study of the Sioux that I discovered one of the old women who made me nice moccasins was also one of the great leaders of the Sioux through the dreadful years of adjustment to reservation life.

The term "Indian Princess" is a fancy of third rate poetry and the show business. Chieftainships were not hereditary; nothing much was among Indians that became less by division. A good family name and the art designs, which belonged to the women, were passed down through the generations. Other things were given away to the needy and the beloved at the death of the owner, the beloved outside of the close relations, of course. The beloved of the tribe were the same as in our society—those who had sacrificed their own advantages for the public good, only the Indians had no commercially colored publicity to mislead him on this. Of course a chieftainship could be revoked at any time and often was; war chieftainships [only lasted] through the warrior years of a man's life, or through misconduct, etc. If [the chieftainship] was one of government or for wisdom, ill health could also bring a revocation or a resigning.

The word "Squaw" was from the Narragansett and never meant "woman" to other Indians except in the whiteman's derogatory sense and therefore was generally considered to be the whiteman's name for *his* woman, who obviously did not have the standing of a woman in Indian society, which was matriarchal. A man left his own people and became one of his wife's upon marriage (and often paid well for the privilege if her family happened to be a good one), the children were her's without argument and all the art forms, such as lodge patterns, the moccasin, quill, and beadwork patterns, etc. When a woman was tired of her man she threw his stuff out of the lodge into the village circle and when he came home and found it there, all he could do was pick it up and take it to his mother's lodge, amid considerable ridicule. He could, too, ask for at least part of his ponies or whatever the pay into the family was back. Sorry I got started on this . . .

In haste,

———

CIRCA NOVEMBER 1948

Editorial Offices
Holiday Magazine
Independence Square
Philadelphia 5, Pa.

Gentlemen:

I want to congratulate you on Donald Wayne's article on the Sioux in the September *Holiday*. It makes me homesick for the old Indian country, but saddens me too, that such a great people is open to the charge of laziness.

No people is by nature lazy. When many individuals of any society become lazy, it is due to some abnormal physical or psychological factor— malnutrition, illness, say, or a sense of hopelessness and futility.

I grew up at the edge of the Pine Ridge country; I know something about the thinness of the Reservation soil, the precipitation that sometimes falls well below the normal of sixteen inches. This is range country, where not even the most energetic white man, with every agricultural knowledge and implement could do more than exist on the shirttail plots owned by the Sioux families.

It is true that the term "lazy Indian" is an old one, and certainly started when some Atlantic seaboard Native came to squat at the supply house of his new neighbors. The term became common around the old trading posts, and, with much government herding, around every windswept agency through the west. It must have received considerable augmentation when the whiteman first saw a Plains Indian village on the move, the able-bodied men spread out ahead and all around the more helpless, their families. In the center the women were loaded down with the dragging travois, the saddle packs, and children. "Lazy bucks!" was the conclusion of anyone who did not understand that in a nomadic hunting society, the men, armed only with bow and spear, must never have a hand encumbered. Game may show up momentarily, or an enemy come charging.

I recall nothing of laziness about the Indian boys and girls I knew in my childhood. The Sioux who work in the steel of the sky scrapers of New York are not hired because they are lazy, and I've heard no one complain from those who fought alongside the Pine Ridge warriors in the last two wars. [. . .]

Give the Sioux a future that an intelligent people can accept as worth some effort, and they'll work.

Sincerely,

———

FEBRUARY 1, 1951

Harold Mantell, Director, Public Relations,
Association on American Indian Affairs,
48 E. 86th Street,
New York, N.Y.

Dear Mr. Mantell:

I am sorry about the program today.[14] I was asked to call Miss Bosley at 11 a.m., and when I got to her she was in a tizzy about the threatening UN broadcast that would cut the program to an hour, only enough for the sponsors. She asked if I wanted to come down and stand by, or come next week.

After saying I didn't care; whatever seemed best to you and her, she asked what I planned to do. There I think I made my mistake. I said I had planned to start by illustrating the two commonest stereotypes with a few gestures and sound, a sort of mimicking—slapping my mouth in a little war whoop, maybe a few movements like an Indian dance step; and then the present Indian, by, while sitting down, make gestures as of braids down my chest and a blanket about my shoulders, draw my mouth down to look vacant: these two notions of Indians are still entertained despite records to the contrary.

Miss Bosley immediately saw this as a production, with an Indian and props, but I wonder if my way, by suggesting the stereotypes, wouldn't be more telling. And it would take less than a minute. From there on I planned to point out how misleading and damaging these two notions of a whole people are, and what the Association is doing and hoping to do to combat them, and what everybody can help to do.

I planned to point out how incompatible the two stereotypes with which I began are—one the "blood thirsty savage" of the past, the other the

I Do Not Apologize

lazy, surly, sneaky Indian, the supposed man of the present. I hope to keep this amusing, but very serious too, through a process of informality—sort of showing and leading on, so not only through the efforts of the Association and the Film Committee, but through everyone who comes in contact with the stereotype, there might be a skeptical reception.

Now I don't know what Miss Bosley wants, and I don't know what you think of any of this. Will you drop me a note if you can make anything out of this hodgepodge?

Sincerely,

————

OCTOBER 3, 1953

Mr. John S. Du Mont,
Greenfield, Mass.

Dear Mr. Du Mont:

I'm very happy to have the picture of you and the three old Cheyennes. Chief Eddie Grey is closely tied in with the Little Wolf and Dull Knife people who made the break north from Indian Territory in 1878, their last rebellion. They were one of the fine, responsible families of the tribe clear back into pre-history.

I am sorry to see that Rufus Wallowing has fallen away so much. He must have been ill. You're right, he knows how to feather his nest, as does every politician, white or red, but these characteristics grow particularly strong in a captive people.

Besides, Rufus knows how many of his people will be hungry this winter, and how welcome a dollar handed out here and there will be. The Cheyennes break my heart—once such a great people, and now, without even decent schools, and four generations of malnutrition.

But thank you for the picture, and something may come of your trip.

Sincerely,

————

FEBRUARY 12, 1955

Annie Laurie Williams,
18 East 41ˢᵗ Street,
New York, N.Y.

Dear Annie Laurie:

Enclosed is a copy of the cast of characters, a synopsis and production notes of the Universal-International's *Chief Crazy Horse*. The original has to be returned to a California friend.

As always, I am astonished at the pointless violence Hollywood commits on historical material. No factually true selection of events could have been less dramatic than what the boys made up for this picture, and along with the loss of drama, they have made a lie of the whole. They not only lost all the dramatic impact of the conflicts within the tribe; with the elements, the times and the white men; and within the man's own mind, but they have committed such shameless libels. By making Crazy Horse's wife the daughter of Spotted Tail, they are making his marriage incestuous in the Indian's meaning of the term. By making the killer of Crazy Horse a breed instead of a white soldier, they are libeling a whole class of people, by calling the breed Little Big Man, they are libeling a whole Indian family. Little Big Man was an Indian, not a breed. He did not kill Crazy Horse, and so on and on. No author would want to charge infringement on his copyright if this is an accurate portrayal of the moving picture. No one would admit putting such a story between book covers, let alone pretending that is was true.

Put this in your files for awhile,

———

MARCH 15, 1954

W.R. Frank Productions,
1040 N. Las Palmas,
Hollywood, California.

Gentlemen:

It has come to my attention that the moving picture of the life of Sitting Bull, the Hunkpapa Sioux leader is to be made not only away from the region in which he lived his eventful life but entirely outside of the country, without utilizing either the background scenery or the background people, the Sioux.

This seems a shocking misuse of our history to me. This exciting and dramatic story of a man you evidently find worth a picture should not be falsified in these essential and readily available elements. No wonder so few pictures based on the American Indian are worth seeing.

A picture on this great Indian leader can be a very tremendous success, financially and dramatically, but not if it is falsified even to the background.
Sincerely,

———

Author: *Crazy Horse: Strange Man of the Oglalas; Cheyenne Autumn*

JULY 20, 1954

Dear Helen Hayes,[15]

I should have answered your letter direct to me here, but I didn't make it and today comes the one forwarded from Wisconsin.

No, the Crazy Horse [movie] is an outright steal, I am told. The Sioux Indians thought it was my story they were working on, because there are things in it that they only told me, they say. From Hollywood I hear that the script was written from my book, but not with pay or with credit. Annie Laurie Williams[16] says we can't do anything until the picture comes out, and then if there are sections that could not have been discovered anywhere except in my book, we will have a case. I suspect it will be another completely phony production, with no connection at all with reality. I'm sorry that they are doing it, mainly because I had a good script man who would have made a good picture of it, eventually.

Love and regrets that Lincoln is so bad—

———

FEBRUARY 24, 1955

Rosebud Yellowrobe[17]
66–23 Yellowstone Blvd.
Forest Hills, Queens, N.Y.

Dear Rosebud Yellowrobe:

It was fine to listen to your sincere and moving talk last night, and to hear of your experiences with the picture *Sitting Bull*.

Because you will certainly be approached for publicity, I am sending you a copy of the synopsis of Universal-International's *Chief Crazy Horse*. The whole miserable distortion is sickening enough, particularly when the magnificent truth is so much more dramatic. The final evasion, however, is making Little Big Man a breed, and having him kill Crazy Horse instead of admitting that a white soldier did the killing. It is the old, old, story—making the mixed blood the scoundrel. In any case, I think the Little Big Man family could sue on this, if they had the money and a good lawyer.

I trust our paths will cross again soon.

————

OCTOBER 21, 1958

Walter Yust, Editor,
Encyclopedia Britannica,
425 N. Michigan Ave.
Chicago 11, Illinois.

Dear Mr. Yust:

I appreciate your letter asking me to revise and condense the article "Lincoln" in the *Britannica*. You do not need anyone with my specialization in Great Plains history for this.

What you do need in the *Britannica* is a long hard look at the treatment of the Indians and the conspicuous white men of the Great Plains. For instance, Sitting Bull is called a "Dakota Sioux" which is erroneous. The Dakotas were the eastern Sioux, of Minnesota, north Iowa and Wisconsin, etc. They had a "D" sound in their language. Sitting Bull was a Hunkpapa, of the Teton or western Sioux, the Lakota, who had no D sound but an "L" instead in their language.

Further on you have this about Sitting Bull: "And during the Civil War he led attacks on white settlements in Iowa and Minnesota."[18] This is a complete lie. Sitting Bull never led an attack on any white settlement anywhere, and never in Iowa or Minnesota. The sentence following the above is also misleading. This connecting Sitting Bull with the eastern Sioux is not a controversial or debatable point but is disproved by even a casual glance into the reports of the Bureau of Ethnology, into Clark Wissler or Stanley Vestal. Even my *Crazy Horse*, chiefly about the Oglala Lakotas makes this division of the Dakotas and the Lakotas clear.

Sorry,

————

Father George
St. Joseph's Indian School
Chamberlain, South Dakota

Dear Father George:

It was fine to see the happy Indian faces when I opened your folder. Even
a familiar name popped out at me—Yellow Elk. There are many cards on
the Yellow Elk family in my index to my Sioux material.

I am taking the liberty of sending your school a copy of my recent little
book, *These Were the Sioux*. I always hesitate about these things. Those of
us outside of the Church never know, although my brothers and I went to
school in the Catholic community on Mirage Flats and Old Jules, my father,
gave ground for the little church there.

I know something of the deprivations of the Sioux children, and I am
grateful for the work you are doing at St. Joseph's. I have just one little
question—why does everyone put those unSiouan head bands on the
girls? These are so reminiscent of the patronizing, sentimental period that
cost the Sioux so much in opportunity and self-respect. I know these head
bands have become customary, but I like to think that the Sioux do not
borrow, but *give* as they gave the war bonnet, which has been taken up by
thousands of Indians who never saw one before the Wild West show days.

I like to see the Sioux girls with the beaded bands hanging from the top
of the braids. These bands meant so much, were so commonly recognized
as the mark of a thoughtful, dutiful, and faithful Sioux maiden and young
woman.

But this is incidental—more important is the opportunity you and the
school are giving to these young people.

Sincerely,

———

JANUARY 20, 1964

Mary Abbot[19]
McIntosh and Otis
18 East 41st, New York, N.Y.

Dear Mary:

Nothing I ever heard about the arrogant tastelessness and rank indecency of Hollywood exceeds the suggestion that I let that corrupt hack, Jack Webb, make a novel of my *Cheyenne Autumn*.

Only the knowledge that Hecht-Lancaster were doing the story from newspaper accounts and that lying book that Howard Fast was hired to write to beat my Cheyenne volume into print ever got me to agree to an uncontrolled sale of a book that contains so much that is sacred to a people.

I find myself in the position of a virtuous woman who foolishly conducted herself so the villain feels free to make his proposition, and in the most off-hand manner, like volunteering to leave a dirty dollar bill on the washstand.

I suspect that there may very well be some Warner trickery, in spite of the prior sale of the book to paperback publication. I still have the correspondence about *Miss Morissa*, which I wrote at the request of Clark at MGM for Greer Garson, who then went to Warners with the outline and made the lady doctor picture for them. While *Morissa* isn't of the caliber of *Cheyenne Autumn*, the story is a masterpiece compared to Warner's *Strange Lady in Town*. I saved all the Clark and Garson letters and the notes on the arrogant letter Jack Warner wrote to Annie Laurie when she reminded him that the woman doctor story was my work, requested for, and by Garson.

Still, it's all material for my autobiography, and I'm just the gal to tell the bald truth.

Sorry—

———

JANUARY 28, 1964[20]

RE: Final script by James Webb for the moving picture made from my book, *Cheyenne Autumn*, completed Fall of 1963, script sent to me June, 1964, for permission to make a novel, to be called *Cheyenne Autumn* from the Webb script.

It seems impossible that this greatest epic of American history could be reduced to a dull, static bore but here is the evidence. The greatest figures are drained of all character—of dignity, force, and integrity. Then there is the incredible insertion of the white girl into the flight. She would have been driven out of camp and from among the fleeing Cheyennes, the Indians whipping her team at every jump. (The only way she could have gone along would have been on someone's race horse, carrying her food, to

I Do Not Apologize

hurry out ahead each time she was driven back, to slip in among the Indians at night or while making their desperate stands, risk the bullet or the arrow of some angry young warrior).

As if destroying the main characters and inserting the girl and her wagon were not enough, dozens of stupid stock cardboard figures have been added: stock soldiers, gamblers, prostitutes and stock senators, only to retard the action, kill the feeble interest aroused. Then there are the endless anachronisms. Plainly none except those completely ignorant of the region or the people would put sabers into the Army of the Plains in 1878 and ignore boundaries of military departments, taking troops from Fort Reno clear to Fort Robinson, when they were turned back at the Platte; put bib overalls on Indians and cries into the mouths of their babies and have Cheyennes spy on bathers. Indians, men, women and children bathed together and were free of the snickering white man attitude toward the human body.

Pointless too, is the false combination of the Sacred Arrows of the Southern Cheyennes with the Sacred Bundle that Little Wolf bore from long before 1878 until it was passed on to another by week long ceremonials years after the flight. Then there is the character assassination of Dull Knife and Little Wolf and their descendants through the fictitious wife-stealing and murder. Dull Knife's wife, Pawnee Woman, could have been dropped from the cast instead of giving her to Little Wolf, making him, by implication, a wife stealer. Encumbering Dull Knife with a fictitious son to steal the wife of his father's great co-leader, Little Wolf, seems overt libel to me, compounded by the spurious killing of this non-existent son by Little Wolf. This is like making a picture in which Madison is given a son to steal the wife of Jefferson, who kills him for it. Those great leaders were white and so protected from such libel. It may be that the Cheyennes are tiring of character assassination too.

All this is Warner Brother's concern, not mine. I can prove by my book that I carried out my responsibilities and obligation to the old Cheyennes who entrusted their stories, rituals, and religion to me, and by my contract with Bernard Smith that I had no voice in the preparation of this script. I prefer to let the matter rest there.

———

JULY 25, 1964

Mr. James R. Webb,
Beverly Hills, California.

Dear Mr. Webb:

I appreciate the time involved in your long letter of July 20 explaining the script of *Cheyenne Autumn*. Unfortunately it explains nothing.

About the sabers: I don't depend upon secondary material like Colonel Todd's *Soldiers of the American Army* when primary sources are available. Back in the 1937–38 period, plowing through the U.S. War Record stored in Washington, I ran across the telegram that went out to all the plains posts in 1873 banning sabers anywhere except for dress parade, sabers admittedly largely discarded as useless weight long before that.

Incidentally, I am just completing the *Battle of the Little Big Horn* for Hanson Baldwin's Great Battles series, a subject that Mr. Baldwin knows I have been studying all my life, most of the research completed before the National Archives staff got their classifying hands on the material. *No sabers* on the Custer trek.

About bib overalls: I went through all the bids for goods issued to both Sioux and Cheyennes on reservations during the seventies. The trousers were all called worsted, but were really shoddy, recaptured wool from waste, old rags, etc. All this came out in the investigations into the graft in Indian contracts. Bib overalls were for artisans and later for hoe men. Not even the cowboys would wear them. When an Indian, during that hopeless period of the 1890s to the first World War, got his hands on a bib overall to cover his nakedness, he cut the bib off and slit them up the front, with his breechcloth underneath.

About the crying Indian children: have you ever seen starving children? Then you know that their crying is silent, as Fitzpatrick knew very well. Army surgeons on the plains remarked in their reports about the silence of the children of the nomadic tribes, taught never to betray their camp to a skulking enemy. As late as Wounded Knee in 1890, when practically every woman of child bearing age had reached maturity under the white man who forbade the old ways, the wounded children did not cry. The keening of the mothers of starving wounded children would have been much more effective in your picture than the fiction of a crying child.

Inserting spurious and momentary conflicts and drama in the picture proves to me that no one bothered to understand the real conflict of the book—the struggle to save some of the young people who might carry the nation on, and the brave hope of teaching them a little of the dignity of the Cheyenne way. [. . .]

The unforgivable section of the picture is the libel on the two great men of the Northern Cheyennes—in the fiction of a Dull Knife son stealing a wife of Little Wolf's, and then the leader killing the youth. True, Little Wolf later, much later, shot a man who had tried to seduce his wife years before and was then, when they were safely back on the Yellowstone, trying to seduce Little Wolf's young daughter. A Cheyenne wife is free to leave her husband, who must bear this with fortitude, but a young daughter must be protected from philanderers. Sober, Little Wolf could never have shot the man, even under this provocation. Sorrowing for those killed at Fort Robinson, and full of the whiskey the soldiers at Keogh gave him to forget, Little Wolf pulled the trigger.

Your concoction is something entirely different. Has it ever occurred to you that you would never have dared take such liberties with the great men of any other minority—not Mexican, Jew, or Negro, but only with the American Indian? Perhaps this will prove the last time for such libel. I hope so.

In the meantime, your face must burn with shame.

———

NOVEMBER 7, 1964

Mr. Henry Morgan,
I'VE GOT A SECRET
WCBS, New York, N.Y.

Dear Henry Morgan:
After years of admiration for your rapier-sharp attack on many of our fallacious public notions, it is disconcerting to find you accepting the sentimental fallacy of large divisions of American Indians as mere provincial tillers of creek bend corn patches.

I realize that there is little prospect of getting any truth about the American Indian to the general public, but it grieves me that you are taken in by so patent a denigration as the common notion that the eastern and southwestern Indians were petty corn farmers, dependent on the vagaries of weather and varmint for existence. Such a mean background did not produce the great Iroquois League, with its statement of confederation that many considered worth some emulation in our Constitution, nor the southwest Indian, who managed to throw off his century-old Spanish yoke for at least a while as early as 1680.

Every informed primary source on the Iroquois speaks of them as Beaver Indians, as dependent on the beaver as the Plains Indians were on the buffalo, and going far beyond the Plains tribes in husbanding their animal reserves. Beaver reserves were carefully tended and harvested, the ownership by families and passed down the matrilineal line. See Horace T. Martin's *Castorologia* (1892, page 140) or the voluminous sources he cites, such as the *Jesuit Relations.* So dependent on the beaver for food were the eastern Indians of whatever tribe, that the early missionaries found the creature a valuable addition to the "Lenten dietary" because otherwise meatless days meant starvation for the Indians, particularly the Lenten season. With pleasant sophistry occasionally necessary to all fixed systems of thought, the missionaries met this emergency by declaring the beaver a fish, because, so they said, he lived on fish.

Meatless times also meant starvation in the southwest. With no beaver in those dry regions, the missionaries obtained special dispensation permitting them and their converts to eat meat during Lenten times because "often there was no other," no other food. As late as 1900 some remote settlements claimed the privilege of meat even for the fast days.

Sometime when you feel like a little mental travel, look up the "youth journeys" of the early American Indians, and the great trading fairs, for the valley of the Annapolis to the mouth of the Colorado.

Sincerely,

———

I Do Not Apologize

4.

The Advocate:
Promotion of
Native Artists
and Writers

———

S   andoz was immensely interested in the arts (with a special concern for writing, of course); this side of her personality comes through in many of her letters in which she describes attending the theatre or a gallery opening in New York or perhaps Denver. But she was especially interested in Native American art and artists, for she believed that they were the best equipped to portray the true stories of themselves. She often advocated for their work to publishers and personally encouraged them to continue artistic endeavor through her correspondence. Sandoz lobbied incessantly for publication of the Amos Bad Heart Bull manuscript and pictographs compiled by Helen Blish. Finally, the University of Nebraska did so, and it is still one of the best books featuring Native American art and artist; Sandoz contributed the introduction to the book even though she was quite ill at the time. *A Pictographic History of the Oglala Sioux* is perhaps one of the most outstanding documentary works in terms of its visual rhetoric, historical record, literary narrative in images, and sheer artistic beauty. It remains a vastly understudied piece, however.

Native American literature and art have always been in existence in one form or another—depictions on winter counts, rock art and pictographs, ledger book records (such as *Pictographic History*), oral narratives, and since the eighteenth century, written works in English. In the late nineteenth and well into the early twentieth century, several American Indian writers began to publish, and their works were met with growing interest among Native and non-Native readers alike. Many were autobiographical works of nonfiction, imbued with rhetorical calls for reform and just treatment for Native peoples. Beginning in the 1940s, however, Native writers' presence in the literary landscape began to diminish—a trend that lasted well into the 1960s and conspicuously corresponded with the trauma of the termination era.

During these particularly bleak years, Sandoz held out a line of support to young and old Native American writers, educators, and artists. She encouraged them to pursue engagement in the arts because she believed that was the venue with an accepting audience. Sandoz recognized the importance of hearing Native voices telling Native stories and histories; she wanted those voices to be heard, and she felt that she might be helpful in some way.

In the aftermath of World War II, American nationalism in the United States saw a marked rise. The general prosperity of the middle and upper classes heralded the improved standard of living, the housing market boom, and the rise in consumer goods. As the economy recovered from the devastation of the Depression and the War years, most Americans wanted nothing to impede their upward mobility. Despite this general prosperity, however, the fracture between the "haves" and "have-nots" increased mightily, and the fracture was most pronounced along color lines. Class tensions and a fear of subversive Communist activity soon riddled the country, becoming their own cultural force of oppression. For example, the House Un-American Activities Committee formed in 1947, and by 1950, the Red Scare was in full swing as the majority of Americans tacitly agreed to freedom restraints and embraced social conformity. Add to this mix the fact that American Indians, in most American minds, did not conform to the American mainstream, nor did it seem that they wanted to. Indians were largely perceived as relics from the misty past, tragic anachronisms, "vanishing," or "all gone." This idea, as we have seen, was heavily promoted in films and other popular media. Additionally, for many non-Indians caught up in the paranoia of the McCarthy years, there was a curious specter of communism in the idea of collective ownership of tribal lands. In fact, *New York Herald* owner-editor James Bennett denounced the Sioux as "Communistic" as early as 1876, following the Custer debacle on the Little Big Horn.[1]

Although many books about American Indians written by non-Indians were on the market during these years, Native writers themselves faced rather bleak opportunities for publication. Only a fortunate few American Indians managed to publish anything on a national level, and some of those only with the help of non-Natives who assisted in the production of their work. The 1950s were especially grim. Osage writer and novelist John Joseph Matthews, Mohawk poet Maurice Kenney, and Powhatan/Delaware scholar and writer Jack D. Forbes were among the lucky ones to get anything into print during these years. Oglala Lakota spiritual man Nicholas Black Elk, with the assistance of white anthropologist Joseph Epes Brown, published *The Sacred Pipe: Black Elk's Account of the Seven Rites of the Oglala Sioux* in 1953. Some of these Sandoz read, but mainly the books in her personal library are written about American Indians. The 1960s were a bit brighter for some Native writers, but only slightly, until 1968 when both N. Scott Momaday's *House Made of Dawn* and Vine Deloria, Jr.'s *Custer Died for Your Sins* changed the direction for Native American literature for all time. But these books, and the surge in Native American writing, wouldn't be in the hands of readers until two years after Mari's death.

The exact reasons for such a lack of Native literary voices during these years can certainly be surmised; there is no doubt that the combination of extremely poor educational opportunities coupled with detrimental federal policies against Native Americans had destructive effects. Augmented by the general distrust of anyone perceived as different from the mainstream, the production and publication of literature by Native writers was nearly impossible. Most American Indians were just trying to survive during these years. Many Americans believed Indians to be ignorant savages who could not be taken seriously as literary artists, and most publishers during these years much preferred the white historian's version of Native history to that of Native people themselves. Likewise, white novelists and writers were much more likely to have their sensationalized "Indian stories" published—though the stories were rarely ever really about Indians; rather, Indians were secondary characters in the larger narrative. Arnold's *Blood Brother* (1947) is a good case in point, as is Thomas Berger's *Little Big Man* (1964). In these books, both of which were later made into sympathetic (and successful) films featuring Native Americans, the main story focuses on white male characters who are "understanding friends" of Indian people. Mainstream America's apathy toward American Indians undoubtedly added to the dearth of Native publishing during these years—it seemed no one cared to know what was going on in Indian country, except for Sandoz and a handful of others.

Native American visual art was in a major transitional status during the years of 1940–1960. Despite the non-interest in real Indians, galleries were exhibiting and collectors were purchasing Native art; but there was a decided imbalance in what was being shown, where it was being shown, and what was bought. Deeply divided on what constituted "authentic" American Indian art, most gallery owners exhibited only pottery, masks, carvings—Kachina dolls were a favorite—and the older the better, for historic antiquities held more value as "primitive art." Like the literary world, the art world preferred to rely on constructs of Native American people, and insisted on certain aspects and characteristics of "real Indian-ness." Numerous non-Indian painters and sculptors of Western themes sold well during this period, often using romanticized and stereotyped representations of Indian people. Both Fredric Remington's and Charlie Russell's work commanded high figures during the period. Ever critical about historical accuracy, Sandoz always managed to weigh in on this issue. She had several friends who were artists, and she recommended that they study the historical record before beginning to paint a Western scene or subject from the past. In a 1952 letter to Major Edward Luce, superintendant of the Custer Battlefield, she intones, "The ideal situation would be the coming together of a good historian and a good artist in one man, but there is no such individual so far as I know."[2] Likewise, she scrutinized to the best of her ability any illustrations that might accompany her writings, and complained when mistakes were made. She was careful in her work and believed others should take the same care to be as thorough—especially where historic cultural representations were concerned. She felt as though many non-Native artists took too many liberties with historic portrayals.

In contrast, American Indian artists were constrained by the prescriptive nature of the marketplace and found their work catalogued and commodified as "folk art" or "crafts." From 1940 and into the late 1950s, the majority of painting considered to be "American Indian" consisted of outlined figures filled in with flat panes of color, and would become known as "Southwest style."[3] Perhaps if trained "properly," a Native artist might find employment as a commercial artist or illustrator for a large company. Native artists who worked in the realm of contemporary art or fine art found that shows and sales were few indeed. Joe H. Herrera (Cochiti Pueblo) was an early practioner in the contemporary modernist art scene, and his work garnered quick criticism because it veered away from the prescribed Indian forms.[4]

Another Native artist, Oscar Howe (Dakota) explored new creative terrain in his painting in the early 1950s as a way to break down the limits imposed on Native art, and met with much resistance to his challenge of the stylistic standards of the "Indian art" establishment. Now recognized as one of the most respected Native American artists of the twentieth century, in the late 1950s Howe's work was stirring up considerable controversy when it was rejected by the annual Philbrook-juried Indian art competition in Tulsa, Oklahoma. Even though he had participated in the individual exhibition just two years prior, the 1958 Philbrook committee did not think his work was "Indian enough." Ruth B. Phillips, Professor of fine arts at the University of British Colombia, relates that "a great empty space gapes in accounts of the history of Native art during almost the entire Modernist century; in standard accounts, the production of 'authentic' and 'traditional' art is perceived to end in the reservation period, while a contemporary art employing fine art media did not begin until the 1960s."[5]

I Do Not Apologize

Indeed, it appears that very few American Indian artists managed to participate in the fine arts before the mid-1960s. Sandoz did not know Howe personally, but there are scattered hints that she knew of his work. She did, however, work with Pawnee artist and illustrator Brummett Echohawk on several of her writing projects, and certainly respected and appreciated his contributions. Sandoz knew that American Indian art was much more than an anthropological curiosity—she understood it as relevant in modern life. Its historic value was of prime importance, but she thought current Native American art and artists deserved fair recognition and to be taken seriously. Sandoz believed that no one was a "born" writer or artist; she knew that anyone who wanted to dedicate time to learning the skills could become accomplished, but she also knew it would take hard work and devotion to each craft. She was, in some ways, a natural teacher; since her younger days as a rural teacher in the sparsely settled area of northwestern Nebraska she had always encouraged people who longed to write. Her correspondence will reveal to future researchers her love of teaching and mentoring of novice writers. The correspondence collection teems with letters to both Native and non-Native writers who sought her advice and assistance in getting their writing published. Two young Native men, Edward Sandcrane and the aforementioned Brummett Echohawk, were recipients of her writing guidance.

Edward Sandcrane was a mere teenager when Sandoz met him in 1949. He was the grandson of Old Sand Crane, the Keeper of the Sacred Buffalo Hat bundle of the Northern Cheyenne tribe in Lame Deer, Montana. A most holy of relics belonging to the tribe and a ceremonial object, the Buffalo Hat bundle was (and is) revered among both the Northern and Southern divisions of the Cheyennes. Although not terribly well educated in the formal sense, Edward showed early talent as an artist and frequently included drawings and stories in his letters to Sandoz during the 1950s. After seeing action during the Korean War as an infantryman in the US Army, Sandcrane applied for the federal relocation program, and for a short while he was employed in Van Nuys, California—far from his Montana homeland. The program did not benefit Sandcrane and before long he returned to the Northern Cheyenne Reservation, quickly renewing his correspondence with Sandoz. The two kept in touch for many years.

There are several features in the correspondence to Sandcrane that I feel deserve special attention. In her letters to Sandcrane, Sandoz tries diligently to persuade him to pursue his dreams of becoming a full time artist. That she cares about him and wants him to succeed is clear; she uses a friendly yet straightforward approach to make her point that his art and stories have importance. One of the motivational strategies we hear in her advice to Sandcrane involves bringing in parallel narratives that have specific historical significance to the Northern Cheyennes. Of special focus is the story of Little Finger Nail, a Northern Cheyenne tribal member who lived during some of the most perilous times of the nineteenth century. Little Finger Nail interested Sandoz for many years; she had found his notebook of drawings mislabeled at the American Museum of Natural History while doing research on the Northern Cheyenne flight from Oklahoma's Darlington Agency. The drawings later became a prominent source used for Sandoz's story of the Sappa fight in *Cheyenne Autumn*.[6]

In the letters she writes to Sandcrane, Sandoz is in a motivational mode and reaches out with stories of the great artist and chronicler of his people, Little Finger Nail. This man was heroic in Sandoz's view because even in his last desperate moments during the ill-fated escape from the prison barracks at Fort Robinson, he tried to protect the ledger and its contents. Though Little Finger Nail was shot and killed, the ledger survived. Sandoz stresses the story to Sandcrane and illustrates how his ancestors were admirable artists, historians, and storytellers—a great people. Here again she seeks to dismantle the stereotypes of the "lazy" or "dirty Indian" that Sandcrane has been deluged with for most of his young life, some of which he may have internalized subconsciously. Sandoz also includes a further show of support by suggesting that she will help make contacts in New York, where he could perhaps sell some of his art. In her best "teacherly" tone, she includes advice about developing his talent as a writer, including stories of her own hardships and sacrifices—certainly an attempt to buoy his spirits. At the close, Sandoz is both supportive and hopeful as she asserts: "Someday your work can be in better places than such magazines. It can be in great galleries, public buildings, in homes of whites and Indians."[7]

Even while Sandcrane was in military service in Korea, Sandoz continued to encourage his storytelling and writing skills. He had previously sent her two stories of the old days, and she was impressed with the content and rhythm of them. She suggests ways he might hone his skills and ways to begin keeping ideas for future projects. A bit troubling, however, is her insistence that he write of "old Cheyennes and old ways."[8] This is somewhat balanced by her suggestion that he also put down his impressions of his current army life as an infantryman. The letter is upbeat and supportive, and Sandoz reminds him that she will gladly evaluate any future writing that he might send to her. Unfortunately, Edward Sandcrane never became a well-known artist or writer. Historian and anthropologist Margot Liberty, who has close ties to the Northern Cheyenne people (and who also corresponded with

Sandoz in the 1960s), relates that Sandcrane died young of alcohol-related health issues.[9]

Brummett Echohawk, a young Pawnee illustrator and commercial artist, also received support and advice from Sandoz. They came to know one another when Echohawk illustrated Sandoz's article "There Were Two Sitting Bulls," for *Blue Book Magazine* in 1949. Afterward, the two developed a long-standing friendship, often visiting together when the opportunity arose. Echohawk, who had served as a combat infantryman in World War II, was from Tulsa, Oklahoma. After his discharge from the service, he found employment as a commercial illustrator for an Oklahoma oil company. Interested in Echohawk's art and writing, Sandoz often corresponded with him to encourage his continuance in both endeavors. She advocated for him to illustrate two of her upcoming works, *The Story Catcher* and *The Horsecatcher*, that were still in the planning stages at that time. Additionally, she recommended him to publishers in an effort to get some of his short stories into print. The tone of her letters to Echohawk is of significant interest, as she is most enthusiastic and complimentary. From her perspective, he had the resiliency and resourcefulness needed to become a respected writer. In her letters, the rhetoric reveals that she is especially keen on his ability to project a certain amount of orality into his prose. She is also captivated by Echohawk's ideas and his insightful use of Indian humor, and the degree to which he includes a subtle psychological study of Indian-white relationships in one of his short stories. She comments, "It is a fine, terse piece, and suggests that you have real talent for a writing career."[10] Rather than the "teacherly tone" she had expressed with Sandcrane, the tone in her missives to Echohawk reveal more of a "helpful colleague" persona. As Sandoz predicted, Echohawk did become a successful artist and writer, who enjoyed a career that spanned several decades. His illustrations and paintings have been well received internationally, and in 1994, he published his book, *Young Rider of the High Plains Country*. Echohawk and Sandoz remained in touch until her death in 1966. Echohawk passed away in 2006, a well-known and internationally recognized artist and writer.

Sandoz was also a staunch advocate for Native American educational opportunities, and often corresponded with institutions that could assist in securing aid for Indian youth. She wrote several letters attempting to secure scholarships and other financial opportunity for Indian students, and had a measure of success for her effort. She firmly believed that with good schooling, American Indian youth would better negotiate and adjust to the conditions of the dominant society. She knew the boarding school system, and felt the practices were abhorrent in most cases because of the abuse and forced assimilation that the children had to endure. Sandoz believed that cultural revitalization and stabilization would be crucial to helping Native Americans situate themselves in modern life. She also understood the desperate need for good Native American educators to teach the young Indian students. In an effort to promote such ideas, Sandoz recommended Ojibwe tribal member Gerry Harvey, a teacher at Birney Day School in Montana, for a John Hay Whitney Foundation scholarship so she could achieve a graduate degree at the University of Wisconsin. Sandoz biographer Stauffer speculates that Harvey may have been one of the first American Indian women to attend graduate school on this type of grant.[11] Harvey was also hailed as the first Native woman to earn her master's degree at the University of Wisconsin.[12] Mrs. Harvey and her husband, Wilbert, taught school on the Cheyenne reservation during the early 1950s; they corresponded often with Sandoz and they became good friends. This friendship gave Sandoz insights to the situation at Birney, Montana, when she could not visit the community personally. It is vital to underscore the fact that Sandoz recognized her responsibility to give back to American Indian communities, and she often inspired and encouraged others to take a similar stance.

Influenced by both *Crazy Horse* and *Cheyenne Autumn*, and through correspondence with the author herself, Peter J. Powell, a young Episcopalian priest, became a researcher of and writer about the Northern Cheyenne tribe in the 1950s. Like Sandoz, he became deeply involved politically as well, assisting American Indian people who were facing the turmoil of the relocation policy during these years. Instrumental in founding the St. Augustine Native American Center in Chicago, Illinois in 1962, Father Powell sought to aid Indian families and individuals attempting to navigate relocation and the urban landscape for the first time. He also lobbied on their behalf in church-related matters, always respectful of the Cheyenne holy ways. Father Powell continues his service to the Northern Cheyennes as of this writing, still makes regular visits to the Montana reservation, and gives aid to urban Indians of Chicago. Powell has published extensively about both the Northern and Southern Cheyennes, consulting with elders and generously dedicating royalties from his books *Sweet Medicine* and *People of the Sacred Mountain* to the tribe. He writes that Mari Sandoz influenced his life "tremendously."[13]

Had there been American Indian Studies programs in the late 1950s and early '60s, Sandoz would have been a strong advocate for them. Interestingly, she managed to influence the field in some ways as it turns out anyway. In 1962, a young anthropology scholar, Raymond DeMallie, began frequent correspondence with Sandoz. DeMallie had read Sandoz's books that portrayed Lakotas and Cheyennes, and he was interested in researching Crazy Horse's Minneconju relative, Touch the Clouds.[14] Sandoz encouraged his interest in Lakota kinship and societal structures and provided him with leads about source materials and other books that might be of help. DeMallie, now a well-known and respected professor of anthropology and founder of the American Indian Studies Research Institute at Indiana University, has published extensively and edited several important works about Lakota life and society. Dedicated to preserving living Native languages, he is presently involved in projects to teach Native linguistics classes in colleges and on reservations.[15] These are just a few examples of the extent of Sandoz's influence through her correspondence.

Sandoz felt that Native Americans deserved equal opportunities in American society as well as serious, respectful scholarly study of their cultures. She sought to encourage development and exploration of these issues when she could. And, as an ally to Native Americans, she understood that their voices should be privileged; their stories and art were *theirs*, and she believed the dominant culture of America should pay attention to these voices. She also believed she had a duty to draw these voices to the attention of anyone who would listen. Sandoz was one of the few American writers of the mid-twentieth century to embrace this concept. And while it is true that she considered herself an "expert" on the Sioux and Northern Cheyenne tribes, she deferred to their own expertise when it came to their stories and art, as the following letters will show.

APRIL 26, 1941

Siyo Miller
801 South Sixth Street
Albuquerque, New Mexico

Dear Siyo Miller:

It was very nice of you to send me Standing Bear's story on Crazy Horse from the Los Angeles Times. Fortunately I have a photostatic copy of it, and because I think you should keep this material for your own Crazy Horse files, I am returning it to you.

[. . .] Mr. Brininstool was still living in California a short time ago. Dr. Hebard of Wyoming is dead. About Grouard: while much of *The Life*[16] is pure journalese, he apparently did live with both Sitting Bull and Crazy Horse, and it is apparently also true that the Oglalas and the Hunkpapas distrusted him.

You and Warcasiwin are right about keeping the Crazy Horse material in the Standing Bear files. It is yours. Some years ago I learned from my work with Mrs. Waggoner and Mrs. Bettelyoun that Standing Bear was gathering material for the Crazy Horse story, so I dropped it for then, conceding his prior claim, and knowing that there was so much greatness in Crazy Horse that not even half a dozen good biographies would capture it all. When Standing Bear died I dropped my Cheyenne book and picked up the Crazy Horse story once more, now to be completed.

In the meantime I don't know how much has been done of Mrs. Bettelyoun's book of her father, James Bordeaux. It is fine material covering the years from around 1840 to 1900, the period of the second great cultural change for the Teton Sioux in 150 years, as seen from one of the traders who were a part of this latter change. But her book was seriously in need of verification, solidification and unification, and while I suggested these things in a general way, and specifically, Mrs. Bettelyoun was around eighty then and couldn't do the work. I carried the manuscript to Boston and the Atlantic Press offered to take it if I would do the necessary work myself. Although I was thoroughly convinced of the importance of recording the story of those days and perfectly willing to give the required year of my life to Mrs. Bettelyoun, I couldn't squeeze out that much time from my own Plains cycle, which will take up every minute of all my possible life expectancy.

I am tremendously convinced of the importance of such material as yours, and my suggestions come for the hope that you would prepare yourself to make the most of it.

Sincerely,

————

MARCH 27, 1950

Mr. Edward Sandcrane,
Birney, Montana

Dear Edward Sandcrane:
Thank you for the fine picture. I am hanging it with my six pictures made by Cheyennes of the Custer fight, and beside one of Chief Little Wolf chasing a Snake Indian.

The Cheyennes have had many fine artists. One of the older time ones, Little Finger Nail, was killed rather young on January 22, 1879, in the escape

I Do Not Apologize

from the barracks prison at Fort Robinson. Perhaps you are related to him. Many people, Cheyennes and whites, have told me about the book he had in which he drew very excellent pictures of his exploits. His friends, Roach Mane or Long Roach and Elk, made some pictures in the book too. This book was supposed to be at the Smithsonian Institution at Washington, but it wasn't. I finally found it in the American Museum of Natural History here in New York. They had it on display in a glass case but it was labeled "Sioux, Artist Unknown." I had such positive identification that they admitted I was right.

There are two bullet holes close together as two finger tips struck through it, made by carbine bullets. There were the shots that killed Little Finger Nail. The book was found on his body up in the last washout fight up beyond Hat Creek bluffs. It was fastened to his waist by belts under his shirt, around on his back, out of the way.

The people who knew him recalled him as a very talented person, a fine singer as well as an excellent artist. Most of the pictures are in color, with the regalia beautifully done, the horses running with excellent action.

The next time I come to the Tongue River Reservation I hope to borrow the book to bring along. Perhaps there will be some who will tell me more about the stories of the pictures to go with the book in the museum case than I can read from them. I know a little about these pictures, and can tell some of the story in them, but not as your people could.

I am sorry to hear that your grandfather has died. I have made a long study of the Sacred Buffalo Hat and the keepers and their responsibilities. I am happy that I saw him before he died.

I hope that your trading post there at Birney grows very fast. There should be a market for the pictures you paint and the crafts too. There is a man here in New York who sells many Indian products. When I get some of the work that must be done now off my hands, I'll go to see him. Perhaps you have contact with him already. If not I'll get his address and what he would like to see.

Sincerely,

———

MAY 9, 1950

Edward Sand Crane
Birney Day School
Birney, Montana

Dear Edward Sand Crane:

I enjoyed the two stories you let Mr. Harvey send to me. They are part of the history of your people and, so that they won't be lost so easily, I have had my typist make you two copies. She tried to make a few corrections in punctuation and grammar so the reading would be easier. Not much, and I hope you will not find the changes incorrect.

Now about yourself: You have been given talent as an artist and as a writer too, I think. In all people, Indian or white or any other, talents are to be used for the people, as the Cheyennes have always known, for a good Cheyenne put the people first. Not that you are not to make a good comfortable life from your talent, but you have a greater obligation even, to make the most of your special ability for your people.

First, I think you will not forget that for any special talent, you must have courage, honesty, practice self denial for the development of your work, and always think of your fellow man in all you do.

Second, you will need to learn the things that go into the ripening of any art, the elementary things like good drawing and composition, use of color, paints, and so on, so you can make the finest presentation of what you wish to show. In the same way learn the things that go into good story writing— spelling, grammar, the meaning and sound of words, and so on.

It will take work. I know. I grew up in the country south of Pine Ridge, on the Niobrara, the Running Water your people knew so well. I went to a country school only a few years and I started to write the old time stories I heard from the Sioux and the Cheyenne friends of my father. I worked my way through the University because there was no money in our home. It took work, and I could not do or have the things that the people around me had, but I would not trade places with any of those people now.

I am sending a copy of *Blue Book*, November 1949, for the library with an article on the two Sioux Sitting Bulls. I am sending this chiefly because the illustrations are by Echohawk, a Pawnee. On the back cover is his picture. You will see how Indian he is.

Some day your work can be in better places than such a magazine. It can be in great galleries, in public buildings, in the homes of whites and Indians, and your stories can be everywhere, and tell us of all the things we should know, and things that we will enjoy.

Good luck—and I am certain that your grandfather's prayers will be with you.

Sincerely,

———

I Do Not Apologize

Maud Houghlan

Dear Maud:

[. . .]

I suppose you are referring to one of the pictures taken at Wisconsin of Geraldine Harvey and me. She happens to live at the same graduate woman's house as I and the University News Service came over for a story and pictures. Gerry is Oneida and Chippewa, a gay, bright energetic Indian girl, as I learned to know Indians around the Sioux. Her husband is a white man, a very interesting man who wants to do something good for young Indians, particularly the artistic ones. I've done a lot of writing to Washington to help keep the two teachers at Birney. Not necessarily the Harveys, although they have plainly done well, it seems, but two teachers. With only one teacher all art and craft work would have to be discontinued, and the writing that has been encouraged. [Wilbert Harvey] has unearthed some very talented ones, like the Sandcranes. They sent me some excellent painting and short writings. With a little encouragement these young Cheyennes could become great descendants of the magnificent Plains people, the old Cheyennes in the pre-agency days. But enough—

[. . .]

Sincerely,

MS

———

SEPTEMBER 27, 1950

Alexander Lesser, Executive Director,
Association on American Indians Affairs, Inc.
48 East 86th Street,
New York 28, N.Y.

Dear Mr. Lesser:

Thank you for sending me a copy of the information on the Opportunity Fellowships, John Hay Whitney Foundation.

This summer, while teaching in the Writers Institute at Wisconsin, I lived in the same graduate women's hall as Geraldine Harvey, American Indian, married to a white man and teaching with him in the Cheyenne schools on the Tongue River Reservation, Montana.

I was familiar with the work of the Harveys and have tried to cooperate with their efforts to develop the abilities of their scholars in painting and writing. I was very pleased to have this closer acquaintanceship with Mrs. Harvey as a person. She is a bright, gay, attractive and yet very studious young woman, ambitious for the Indians. So far her education (including the Masters earned this summer) has been too concentrated on work in elementary schools. Fortunately she has much wider interests and is eager for wider horizons for herself and the people with whom she works. A former teacher of hers tells me she is very stimulated by the sociological history of the American Indian and the self advancement efforts and opportunities of minority peoples. I found her eager for wider knowledge in these fields, passionately, and humorously anxious to bring wider outlooks and opportunities to the Indian people.

I think Geraldine Harvey would profit very much from an Opportunity Fellowship from the John Hay Whitney Foundation, and surely the Indians would profit even more, as well as the rest of us.

Sincerely,

———

FEBRUARY 5, 1951

Pvt. Edward L. Sandcrane,
RA19392138,
Co.I, 1ˢᵗ Inf. Regt.
Fort Ord, California

Dear Edward Sandcrane:

It's nice to hear that you are managing to do a little work on your art in the army. The Harveys wrote that you had gone into the service, and clippings that friends of mine at Miles City sent me from the agency news columns in the papers included your name and your picture.

I am sorry too, as you are, that Mr. Harvey went into newspaper work. I suspect that he'll regret it too some day. He was very much interested in bettering the lot of the Cheyennes and it is sad to lose any man like that. I recommended Mrs. Harvey for a Whitney Fellowship for further study in college and for a survey of the educational facilities at Tongue River. I think we might get a Whitney fellowship for you to study art some day if you get enough painting done to show that you have a genuine talent, as I think you have. The Whitney fellowships were created to give talented young Indians and other under-privileged minorities a chance to develop their abilities. I'm enclosing a copy of the information sheet for you. Think about it a little.

I am going to be on television next Wednesday for a short talk on the need of showing the American Indian as a human being in the newspapers, the movies, and on television—not as a stereotype (usually a blood-thirsty warrior or stupid agency sitter). Indians will have to be pictured as people with all the dreams and hopes and aspirations, and all the abilities and capacities that are the gift to all human beings. Then they will be treated as human beings.

Will you have a place to save your painting? And do you plan to try writing any of the old Indian stories you remember from the Old Cheyennes? Perhaps in thinking them over, or telling them to the other men in the army, they will become fresh in your mind again. I wish you would write them down and save them. Some day you can work them over, polish them. And your adjustment to army life and the places you will be going the next three years—why not put these impressions down too? I shall be interested in seeing anything you might wish to send me.

And give my regards to your people when you write to Birney.

Sincerely,

————

APRIL 15, 1951

Dear Elizabeth Otis:[17]

Enclosed is a carbon of a brief of a talk I'm to make April 18. As I prepared the material for my talk it occurred to me that there might be a market for an article implicit in the last three paragraphs of the brief. If you are interested let me know.

The American Indians still succeed better than any other racial or national group in our country to orient their young people socially and individually. This is done without whipping or physical restriction but by precept, example and the natural learning from mistakes.

From birth the child becomes aware of his obligations to his fellows and of his security in his claim on their allegiance, love and assistance. Much of their pattern of teaching has a humorous slant.

For instance they will tell you that it is well known that the eldest son needs a second father, "so he won't be around all the time, making the old man feel he's being crowded out of the nest by the fat young bird." The eldest son also needs a second mother and "the woman who will not find one for her first born son better throw him into a snow bank at birth so she will not make a fool of herself over him, and a fool of him—"

Also it is well known that the young husband becomes a part of his wife's people, but to show his respect for her mother he can never address her except through a third person and she must show the same respect for him. The only case of mother-in-law trouble I ever knew among Indians was one of an affable Sioux who got a divorce from his wife so he could go sit for his long visits with her mother as he did during the courtship. The day of the divorce he came to the mother's house with the divorce papers in his hand. He said, as he settled himself, "Now we can talk as friends once more!"

But the important things are implied on page four. These could be made into a short article of say 4000 words, or treated as two articles—one on boys, one on girls.

Sincerely,

———

JUNE 4, 1951

The Ford Foundation
575 Madison Avenue
New York, N. Y.

Gentlemen:

From the *New York Times* of June 3, 1951, I get a fine picture of the tremendous work outlined by the Ford Foundation. I am particularly pleased with the provisions made to facilitate college work for exceptional young people from the high schools. From my annual summer connection with the University of Wisconsin,[18] I know the program there will be well and enthusiastically executed.

Because of my interest in opportunities for young people, and my familiarity with the lack of opportunities for the young American Indians, I wonder if there might not be some provision in your plans for them. The economic situation on most reservations is so bad that few Indians can hope to finance even tuition for their sons and daughters, and the schools are so inadequate that scholarships are practically unavailable to the few who finish high school.

I am enclosing a brief of a talk I gave before the annual meeting of the Association on American Indian Affairs recently, and a subsequent letter published by the *New York Herald*, both of which touch on this subject, among other things.

I Do Not Apologize

You are to understand that there is nothing I want for myself in this, beyond the privilege of calling something of the Indian's situation to your attention.

Sincerely,

————

JUNE 9, 1952

Mr. Brummett Echohawk
12 East Haskell Place
Tulsa, Oklahoma.

Dear Mr. Echohawk:
Of course I remember you as the illustrator of "There Were Two Sitting Bulls," as soon as I saw the return on your envelope.

I don't need to tell you how happy it makes me to have people like you find some satisfaction in my writing. Thank you. And I am happy to know that you had so intelligent an upbringing.

And, I am glad to have your address. I don't know if you are interested in doing illustrations for juveniles, but for years I've been putting off two biographical books for the 12–16 age groups on Cheyenne individuals.

Both were men who excelled in something besides fighting. I won't get at these for another six months perhaps, but I do want to know what you think. The period, in one at least, is 1840 to about 1850, on the plains, of course. Horses and hunting and history-keeping will be important. Since these were important in Pawnee life as well, you would have a feeling for all this.

I am only at Wisconsin during their 8 weeks summer Writers Institute, in charge of advanced fiction writing.

Sincerely,

————

JULY 28, 1952

Mr. Joseph Flute
Box 23, Sisseton, South Dakota

Dear Mr. Flute:
Today I received your letter of October 8, 1951 to Oliver LaFarge, of the Association on American Indian Affairs, East 86th Street, New York. In this

letter you inquire where your uncles, who scouted for the white soldiers under General Sibley in the outbreak of 1862 were stationed.

Most of the scouts were enlisted on regular scout rolls. Most of these found their way to Washington, D.C. and are now in the National Archives there, in the War Records division. To trace them I need the names of your uncles, in English, and also in Dakota or Lakota if you have them. Sometimes in those earlier days the enlistments were in Indian only. There were, of course, less formal enlistments too, nothing more than hiring men out to scout a day or two, to be paid out of a scout fund or sometimes by the officer himself, not the government. If the Indian was paid by the government as a duly enlisted scout often he was entitled to a pension later. Many men did not understand this and never applied for the pension or had difficulty getting it approved, particularly if they were transferred to another agency where their war record could not be sworn to by eye witnesses.

If you will write me the names of your uncles, I'll try to track them for you through Washington.

Sincerely,

————

DECEMBER 7, 1952

Brummett Echohawk,
12 East Haskell Place,
Tulsa, Oklahoma

Dear Brummett Echohawk:

It was so fine to meet you, and to discover that you are the kind of young Indian that the Old Ones of your tribe would certainly approve. Too bad about your buck—but better fortune next time. It reminded me of a story Old Pawnee told us on his way home to Oklahoma from the Brules, about a buck that carried his only arrow and wouldn't lay down to die. The snow was beginning to run again as the wind picked it up. It's vague in my mind now, how he finally got the meat and dug into the snow and next day got back into camp, but I recall the feeling of excitement as he told it in his sketchy English and with fine gestures.

I've been planning to write you about the Indian book for which I should like to have your illustrations. (The final decision in these things always lies with the publisher, as you know). My contracts and commitments get thicker instead of clearer, with my agent talking me into another book on the buffalo days, white man. I should have preferred to do the Indian book because I like to alternate my work, and I do feel I owe a great personal debt, philosophically, to the Plains Indians.

The book you refer to is, I think, *The Fighting Norths and Pawnee Scouts*, by Robert Bruce, published with the cooperation of the Nebraska State Historical Society, in Lincoln. The last I knew there were a few copies left but that was long ago. If not, then try rare book dealers in your region. If that fails, you might try a friend of mine, South Pass Pete Decker, who is greatly interested in Western Americana.

And I wish you a good holiday season and the best New Year under the Great Sky.

Sincerely,

———

P.S. I intended to have you take your magazines when you were here, but unless you need them, I shall keep them. There's no telling when an opportunity to give your name to a publisher might come up.

February 12, 1954

Dear Rufus Wallowing,

I am happy that you and Mrs. Wallowing and your friends like what I tried to do in *Cheyenne Autumn*. It's nice to please the critics but I much prefer to have those who know the region and the people feel that I have not failed too badly.

Yes, you are right. There is a good book in the story of the Cheyennes in the north from the fall of 1876 to the present. I know something about Sweet Woman, White Bull, Two Moons and so on but you are so closely tied to this through Two Moons, who is very prominent in this story, so why don't you do it? Oh, I know you are not a professional writer but a flavor of the Indian way of telling the story would be good. Why don't you gather all the material you can and with the help of your nephew, Jimmy King, put it into an early draft. You are welcome to send me some of the early sections for advice as you go along, if you like. (I have taught the advanced writing courses at the University of Wisconsin every summer for the last seven years; I'm supposed to know how to help people become writers.)

Naturally, at first the writing will be stiff and awkward. That's true in any art, but with practice it will improve. I'll be glad to do a little polishing on the book when you've finished it, if you like, as a neighbor would help out another. I've always regretted that so few Indians have written their own stories. I finally got a Pawnee started at the story of his own people, but not a Sioux or a Cheyenne so far. Of course there was Luther Standing Bear long ago, but he didn't go back very far.

Why shouldn't you be the first Cheyenne to do a book about your people?

Good luck,

———

APRIL 10, 1954

Mr. Brummett Echohawk,
537 North Cheyenne
Tulsa, Oklahoma

Dear Brummett Echohawk:
Thank you for the copy of your story, "The Man Who Scratched Himself." It's a fine, terse piece and suggests that you have the talent for a real writing career. I do wish you could have managed the drawing of the easterners in the buggy so the driver would have been on the right side for team driving, but the cut had to lead the eye inward in the make-up. Your humor, and your understanding of the psychology of Indian-white man relationships are excellent.

Incidentally, have you the new George Hyde book on the Pawnees? He hates Indians, but he often digs up useful information, nevertheless. His *Red Cloud's Folk* is a valuable book in all but his findings from the evidence. The evidence is usually reliable.

I look forward to a lot of fine writing, well illustrated, from you. Don Ward said you were in to see him. I think your writing is aimed for markets beyond the outright action story. There is no reason why you can't do stories for the *Atlantic*, and with your wry humor, *The New Yorker*—and good books, too.

Your "Scratch" story is far above the usual material in Sunday supplements. Did I write you about noticing your drawing on the All American Indians Days folder?

Sincerely,

———

Mrs. Margot Pringle Liberty,[19]
Birney Day School,
Birney, Montana

Dear Margot Liberty:

I am happy to hear from you but disturbed by what you write of Eddie Sandcrane. Of course I knew he would have a very difficult time. If he had even a high school education one might work out some sort of program but as it is the problem is a difficult one. If he had the confidence of the Cheyennes in, say the 1830s or 1840s it could be done, but he is the victim of generations of betrayal, degradation, disease and malnutrition. Now, on top of all the rest, comes the color discrimination, something non-existent in my childhood. With the shrinking cattle prices, jobs are scarcer and the Indian is the first man out.

Yet, with his talent, Eddie could, if he believed in himself and were willing to put in the work, the apprenticeship that his talent is worth, he could make a good artist of himself. If he had the educational qualifications he would be accepted as an equal in any art department. Several Indian artists have been happy developing their work at Dakota Wesleyan, just to mention one place. Hasn't he any G.I. Bill training coming?

I think a large city like New York would be a hopeless place for him. I know half a dozen Indian artists here, some who came here with some reputation and good sales behind them. The only one who was able to adjust himself was Brummett Echohawk, and he had the sense to go back to Oklahoma to an oil company drawing job. It's not what one could wish for an artist but at least he's not defeated.

My best advice (and I know so little of the situation that I know that it's worthless) would be to get any and every bit of training the G.I. Bill will give him, and get at it as soon as possible. Then he should put in all his spare time in work on his craft work too. I suppose one of his problems is getting materials. That, if his work is good, will overcome itself. Buyers will furnish him with leather, copper, wood, etc. for the work they want when he has established his ability to do good work and his dependability.

Did you meet Father Powell at Sheridan last summer? (I couldn't come; as always I was teaching at the University of Wisconsin). I'm sending a few quotations about Eddie from your letters to him. He works with a group of Indians at Chicago, and there is a growing strength in them, I understand, both for themselves and to help others.

Eddie has relatives down in Oklahoma. There the Cheyennes manage considerable marketing of their arts and crafts. Perhaps he could get leads from them. It's so much a problem for him—the need to say "I can and I will," but that's a difficult thing for Indians now. I believe that Eddie Sandcrane is one who could learn to do this as his grandfather did.

Sincerely,

———

MAY 25, 1957

Reva Edwards, Editor,
The Gordon Journal,
Gordon, Nebraska.

Dear Reva:

Thank you for your fine spread of pictures of Emmett American Horse, and his family too, at Lincoln. I hope to see the time when more and more young Sioux can get the opportunity to make the most of the greatness that lies in their heritage, not only in the athletic prowess and in the fleetness of their runners, but also in their organizational talents and their artistic and philosophical genius.

Gordon can be proud that these young men are being given their opportunity there. The American Horse brothers can be proud that they are contributing to the continued eminence of one of the most honored Sioux families from clear back in the old buffalo hunting days.

Best wishes,

———

JULY 27, 1957

Rufus Wallowing
Lame Deer, Montana.

Dear Rufus Wallowing:

I'm happy to hear from you, and sorry that you and Mrs. Wallowing aren't in perfect health. It's typical of you that you face the little aches with a philosophical calm.

You say that you disagree with one item in my *Horsecatcher*, the snake eating. I got my information from good authority but because there are different attitudes and usages among different branches of every tribe, I should like to know what you have to say on this.

Incidentally, you should write down as much of the old lore as you recall. When such men as you are gone there will be no one to do this, and much that is interesting and valuable because it was wise will be lost forever. Perhaps I can help you get some of this published.

I was on the Martha Deane radio program, KFOR, Mutual Broadcasting Company, talking for the Indians last week. I realize that these things help very little but I feel I must help the little I can to get some understanding for the Indians, both for their contributions and for what they can contribute to our wisdom, and for some interest in their present unhappy situation.

It is good to know that you have a start with one little factory on the reservation. If this is successful there can be more to give the people some cash income, something useful for their time.

Father Powell of Chicago tells me he is coming through Lame Deer this summer. He will look you up, I think. He made a good talk to the Chicago Westerners last winter about the Indian situation, which was published.

I wish all of you a fine fall and winter, and do send me anything you write and wish me to look over. Longhand is alright.

Sincerely,

————

JULY 14, 1960

Hila Gilbert,[20]
961 Delphi,
Sheridan, Wyoming

Dear Hila Gilbert:

The plans for the LITTLE FINGER NAIL CHEYENNE ART AWARD[21] for work by an artist of the Northern Cheyennes sounds fine. If this works out well, I shall see that there is another 25.00 for next year, and thereafter so long as the results and the handling of the award seem to justify its continuation. Perhaps others might eventually add to this little start and make it worthwhile.

I am thinking of establishing a similar award for the Oglalas of Pine Ridge, if I can find a good group interested in the sponsoring of the arts and crafts there, a group free from the pressure of local cliques.

Good luck—in the Cheyenne sense of the term,

————

AUGUST 3, 1961

Eugene L. Price, Editor
The Beacon
Ohio Oil Company
Findlay, Ohio

Dear Gene Price:
Your book with Brummett Echohawk sounds fine. I've met Brummett
and like both him and his work. I wish he could find time to do the kind of
book the Pawnees should have, one that makes a coherent whole of their
religion, philosophy, and life as it was when the white man's influence first
came. I realize that this will be difficult, and will demand much peeling off
of adopted practices and attitudes, but Brummett is the man to attempt it.
Perhaps some of his tapings are aimed in this direction.
[. . .]
Sincerely,

———

NOVEMBER 27, 1961

Bruce Nicoll, Director
University of Nebraska Press
Lincoln 8, Nebraska

Dear Bruce:
Enclosed is a carbon of my letter to Harvey Little Thunder with some of
the sources for material on his ancestor, Little Thunder, attacked by Harney
at Ash Hollow, more correctly across the Platte on Blue Water Creek.
Harvey's wife was Trudy Bordeaux, apparently a grand niece of Susan
Bordeaux Bettelyoun. Both of the Little Thunders grew up on Rosebud
Reservation. They are attractive and well-spoken. Perhaps you can get some
action on the Bettelyoun manuscript, and additional background material
through them.
Incidentally, there's a fine biography in old Little Thunder, and if you find
someone to do it (perhaps Harvey, who has some education) there's much
more material in my files. I'll turn the whole index over to your biographer.
Also, I still think you might consider a book published in the 1930s,
written by a Negro woman from a settlement in South Dakota. I remember

I Do Not Apologize

enjoying the book, but I don't recall author, title or publisher—how's that for a bad reporter?

Perhaps the Reverend Mr. Stith, teaching in the Lincoln Schools, Lefler Junior High, I think, might do a book on his home community, the Negro settlement in Cherry County, where he was born. He was a naval chaplain in World War II, etc. The Historical Society should have his material.

————

JANUARY 3, 1963

Walter Frese[22]
[Hastings House Publishers]

Dear Walter:

There is a fine book in the story of Brummett Echohawk.

I've not heard that the University of Oklahoma Press or anyone else has tied him up with a contract. Probably the usual contempt for the nearby has prevented Oklahoma from seeing the value of the story, or perhaps the fact that Brummett is an Indian.

The story is so much in keeping with the tradition of Plains warrior conduct. I don't know the authenticity of the details of this story, but that would be easy to check. I do know that the Indian units, Pawnee, Cheyenne, and some others were practically slaughtered to nothing in the Italian landings. Only the Indian morale kept them from breaking when the casualties rose far above acceptable percent for modern warfare.

Brummett's war wounds are beginning to tell, I hear, and giving him considerable trouble. But he still does covers, etc. for oil company publications and such.

Write him if you're interested. I sent him a note to remind him that he should be putting the book together, but I didn't mention a publisher.

Sincerely,

————

JANUARY 15, 1963

Brummett Echohawk
Tulsa, Oklahoma

Dear Brummett:

I should like to put together an outline for your book but that's a lot like arranging a composition for a picture that you are to paint—which could not help but be completely alien to your concept and perhaps violate your idea of both art and spirit.

Still, I'll risk some suggestions which may serve as stimulation or irritation, also a useful spur to artistic ends, sometimes. I should make the book scrupulously factual and true, within the limits of the story as I knew it. I should start with the Pawnees fighting in Italy, getting in some bits of Pawnee war strategy, observation of the terrain, with the deductions, maneuvering, the fading into the landscape. You will know this far better than anyone else. I should be inclined to go through your story by this method until your hospitalization. And then, with your fever, and impatience with the waiting, you could include references back to your ancestors (am I correct in recalling that you have a connection with the Pawnee Scouts?) and their exploits. Add anything here that you find pertinent and dramatic: rituals, village life, fights with other tribes as well as the action of the Pawnee Battalion. Work the reader up to such a pitch that he is with you when you start back to the front, flying instead of riding one of the excellent Pawnee horses.

Where you end the story is for you to decide. Make it a good high point . . . don't let it dwindle to an anticlimax.

Your story, well told, will be on a sort of two levels by this kind of plan, the first section the contemporary story on the surface, with underneath the suggestions of a warrior Pawnee ancestry. The middle section, the old Pawnee fighters, with the undercurrent of your slow mend from the critical injuries, and the third part once more the modern Pawnees, you in the foreground, with the old timers in the undercurrent their qualities living on in the fighting Pawnees of World War II.

Don't worry about a good beginning. Just start writing. Everyone expects to throw away the beginning later and then, when the book is nearing completion, writing the beginning that is right for the book. If you find it easier, write up incidents here and there in the story and put them together later. [. . .] Write the string of the story, making it move. Later, you can fill in the descriptions, characterization, dialogue, etc. of the Italian fight and of the old time ones, including the weather, powder smoke, etc. Tell the story in first-person, check on the old timer's accounts for dates and through documents etc. You'll have to determine where the truth lies and the discrepancies.

Don't worry about your writing in the first draft. Get the story down and polish it later. I make many revisions of every page of writing, although I've had seventeen books published. [. . .] I think this book should be nonfiction, keeping to the actual characters and events, telling the truth as you see it. Collect photographs and maps; most nonfiction carries photographs if the subject is some period after the camera reached the region, and even items that you think might photograph usefully for illustration.

Well, there's more than one way to write a book. Good luck!

Sincerely,

—————

NOVEMBER 21, 1965

Jane L. Pope, Consultant
Nebraska Public Library Commission,
Lincoln, Nebraska 68509

Dear Jane Pope:

It was fine to see you and to bask a bit in the breath of western air you brought with you.

I've been thinking about the Sioux and Valentine and I wonder if I might make a sort of collateral suggestion. I should like to have someone work with the young Sioux in one of the fields in which they naturally excel. The readiest, I suspect, is art, and I wonder if there is anyone around Valentine who would undertake an art contest for the Indians, with prizes in various categories, small, of course, and even in-store credits if necessary.

The work could include various fields from black and white, crayon, and pastel through water color and oil and even murals, and include adults down to children. Surely there is some empty space where the show could be put on, with time enough for the entries for new work, and a show open long enough so many could come to look. If there is library space for the show, all the better—

Happy Holidays to everyone—

—————

Mari Sandoz at either a book signing or a dinner in her honor. Photo appeared in the *Omaha World Herald*, June 5, 1958. Caroline Sandoz Pifer Collection, Mari Sandoz High Plains Heritage Center—Chadron College. 2003.001.00340.

Afterword:
The Alongsiders

O   ut in northwestern Nebraska among the seemingly endless grass-covered Sandhills, a solitary dark granite headstone marks Mari Sandoz's grave. It's far from the beaten path where only a dedicated few will dare to visit. But once there in that landscape one becomes acutely aware why Sandoz wrote of her region and the diverse people who were, and are, its denizens. There is an openness of earth and sky that allows the mind respite and freedom. I think it fitting that she rests there, a sort of guardian sentinel of those Sandhills; occasionally one will notice a tobacco tie or two left there in her honor. But those are not the only indications that American Indians have taken notice of her contributions as an ally.

The introduction to the 2004 edition of Sandoz's masterpiece, *Crazy Horse: Strange Man of the Oglalas*, was written by the venerated Native American scholar and intellectual, Vine Deloria, Jr. His position as one of the most respected American Indian thinkers and activists will remain unchallenged for many years. An outspoken critic of non-Indian researchers and writers who make their careers as "experts," on American Indian subjects, Deloria has written on such diverse topics as American Indian treaty law, sovereignty issues, education, technology, and religion. His best known work, *Custer Died for Your Sins*, first published in 1968, cleared a path into Native studies like nothing else had done before; it continues to inspire people the world over. So I wondered, when I found that he had written an introduction to my favorite of Sandoz's books, if he liked it. He did. In fact, he praises the book as a work that stunned him "[with] the wealth of detail contained in each line of text—material that must have come from her conversations over time with a large number of elders . . . and later woven into a chronicle of the times that overflows with authenticity."[1] This is indeed high praise coming from someone who dedicated his life to writing about and promoting American

Indian rights. This is not to say that Deloria thought the book was perfect. He had some arguments with it, but in the main he writes that Sandoz wrote with feeling and nuance that only few would know or understand, and he takes a last salvo at the critics who are still dismissing her work today:

> How unfortunate that reviewers and scholars lacking any experience of the western lands have missed the real genius of the book. Although it has withstood the test of time, it has not received the acclaim that it is due. Perhaps it speaks primarily to those people who, like Sandoz, have their roots in the plains and their peoples. Or perhaps it is the careful reader who savors the well-written word who can see in this book history as biography and biography as history.[2]

This may seem like the ultimate endorsement of Sandoz's research, writing, and storytelling, but Sandoz still has many critics who would disagree. And that is healthy for the field of Native Studies—we need more discussion, debate, and conversations to center ourselves on making new knowledge. But it is my hope that, in a time when positionality in this field of study seems to be stratified into "insiders" and "outsiders," perhaps we can make room for those "alongsiders," like Mari Sandoz—writers and researchers who approach to listen first, and write responsibly and respectfully as advocates and allies. It seems to be possible if we can learn from those who've gone before, Native and non-Native, and come to some kind of intellectual kinship and compassion in which we can foster solidarity in honoring treaty rights. It certainly seems to be the goal Sandoz worked toward during her lifetime, as the letters attest.

The letters presented in this volume are only a fraction of those available for research in the Sandoz Collection. Letters of this magnitude may never again be produced on paper given technological advances in digital and electronic communications. Sandoz's letters and the period of time they represent stand as a repository of information that is unique, useful, and deserving of study. This book and Helen Winter Stauffer's book, *The Letters of Mari Sandoz*, are really only the tip of the iceberg for anyone serious about the study of Great Plains writers, or non-Native writers who engage in research about American Indians. This intersection merits attention from Native scholars and non-Native scholars alike because Sandoz was one of the first writer-historians to realize and understand the serious situations American Indians were facing during the tumultuous years of the mid-twentieth century. She wrote with respect for and responsibility to the tribes, and advocated for their rights as the U.S. treaties ordained.

RECIPIENT LIST

NOTES

PLAINSWORD

1. "Song of the Plains: the Story of Mari Sandoz," NETV, Lincoln, NE, 1978.

2. See John R. Wunder, "Writing of Race, Class, Gender, and Power in the American West: Mari Sandoz, Precursor to the New Indian History," in Raili Poldsaar and Krista Vogelberg, eds., *North America: Tensions and (Re)solutions*, Cultural Studies Series No. 8 (Tartu, Estonia: University of Tartu Press, 2007), 266–83.

3. "Song of the Plains," 1978.

4. Ibid. See also Ron Hull–Mari Sandoz interview, KUON-TV, April 1972.

5. Helen Winter Stauffer, *Mari Sandoz: Story Catcher of the Plains* (Lincoln: University of Nebraska Press, 1982), 1–10, 229–61.

6. Ibid., 11–33; John R. Wunder, "Some Notes on Mari Sandoz," *Prairie Schooner* 80 (Winter 2006): 42–45.

7. Stauffer, *Mari Sandoz*, 80–81, 151–53.

8. See Mari Sandoz, *Crazy Horse: Strange Man of the Oglalas* (New York: A. A. Knopf, 1942); *Cheyenne Autumn* (New York: McGraw-Hill, 1953); *These Were the Sioux* (New York: Hastings House, 1961); and *The Battle of the Little Bighorn* (Philadelphia: Lippincott Co., 1966).

9. See Mari Sandoz, "There Were Two Sitting Bulls," *Blue Book* (November 1949): 58–64; "The Search for the Bones of Crazy Horse," *Westerners Brand Book* [New York Posse] (Autumn 1954): 4–5; "Introduction," *The Cheyenne Indians: Their History and Ways of Life* by George Bird Grinnell (New York: Cooper Square Publishers, 1962); "Introduction," *A Pictographic History of the Oglala Sioux* by Amos Bad Heart Bull and Helen Blish (Lincoln: University of Nebraska Press, 1967); "The Far Looker [An Indian Tale]," *The Sight-Giver* (February 1939), n.p.; "What

the Sioux Taught Me," *Empire* 24 (February 1952), reprinted in *Reader's Digest* (May 1952): 21–24; "Some Oddities of the American Indian," *Westerns Brand Book* [Denver Posse], 1955, pp. 17–28; and "The Great Council," compiled by Caroline Sandoz Pifer (Gordon, NE: Gordon Journal Press, 1970).

10. See Mari Sandoz, *The Horsecatcher* (Philadelphia: Westminster Press, 1957) and *The Story Catcher* (Philadelphia: Westminster Press, 1963).

11. See John R. Wunder, "Mari Sandoz: Historian of the Great Plains," 97–135; Suzanne Julin, "Annie Heloise Abel: Groundbreaking Historian," 45–63; Shirley A. Leckie, "Angie Debo: From the Old to the New Western History," 65–95; and Patricia Loughlin, "Alice Marriott: Recording the Lives of American Indian Women," 209–41. All in Shirley A. Leckie and Nancy J. Parezo, eds., *Their Own Frontier: Women Intellectuals Re-Visioning the American West* (Lincoln: University of Nebraska Press, 2008).

12. Vine Deloria, Jr., "Introduction," to Mari Sandoz's *Crazy Horse: Strange Man of the Oglalas* (Lincoln: University of Nebraska Press, 2004), vii.

13. See Helen Winter Stauffer, *Letters of Mari Sandoz* (Lincoln: University of Nebraska Press, 1992).

INTRODUCTION

1. Mari Sandoz , letter to Mamie Meredith, 1943. Mari Sandoz Collection, Don L. Love Memorial Library, University of Nebraska–Lincoln.

2. This is a term coined by Native scholar Gerald Vizenor (Ojibwe), and used to denote a concept of survival through resistance. It is a term used frequently in Native American studies and literature.

3. "Dedication of Sandoz Sandhills Trail held March 24," *One Drop: Mari Sandoz Heritage Society* Newsletter, Fall 2001.

4. This is a personal term I often use to describe those interested in Mari Sandoz and her writings.

5. Helen Winter Stauffer, *Mari Sandoz: Story Catcher of the Plains* (Lincoln: University of Nebraska Press, 1982), 23.

6. Stauffer, *Mari Sandoz: Story Catcher of the Plains*, 27.

7. Sandoz did return to live in the family home briefly just before the publication of *Old Jules* in 1932, and in fact drafted the majority of *Slogum House* while living at the ranch.

8. Mari Sandoz, *These Were the Sioux* (New York: Hastings House, 1961), 17.

9. Stauffer, *Mari Sandoz: Story Catcher of the Plains*, 134. See also Mari Sandoz to Edward Weeks, 2 February 1940.

10. Mari Sandoz to Miss Eleanor Hinman, 1 March 1940.

11. Mari Sandoz to President Harry S. Truman, 18 October 1949.

12. Mari Sandoz to W. Houlton, 19 September 1951.

13. Stauffer, *Mari Sandoz: Story Catcher of the Plains*, 81.

14. Caroline Sandoz Pifer spoke with me about this in 1999, and again in 2003, saying that some information Mari had concerning Crazy Horse and his family relationships was destroyed at the time of Sandoz's death as she had instructed.

15. Mari Sandoz, *Cheyenne Autumn* (Lincoln: University of Nebraska Press, 1992), 268.

16. Mari Sandoz, *Crazy Horse: Strange Man of the Oglalas* (New York: Hastings House, 1970), 413.

17. This maybe the unnamed article Sandoz referred to in the letter to Houlton, but the evidence is unclear.

18. D'Arcy McNickle, *They Came Here First* (Philadelphia: J. B. Lippincott Co., 1949), 93.

19. Donald L. Fixico, *Termination and Relocation: Federal Indian Policy, 1945–1960* (Albuquerque: University of New Mexico Press, 1986), 94.

20. Sandoz to W. R. Frank Productions, 15 March 1954.

CHAPTER 1

1. Richard Voorhees, "Professor Fling 'Difficult' but Essential to Mari's Historical Methods," *One Drop: Mari Sandoz Society Commemorative Issue* (Spring 2003): 8-9.

2. Betsey Downey, "'She Does Not Write Like a Historian: Mari Sandoz and the Old and New Western History," *Great Plains Quarterly* (Winter 1996): 9-25.

3. Mari Sandoz to *Atlantic Monthly Press,* 5 October 1932.

4. Voorhees, "John D. Hicks and Mari Sandoz," *One Drop: Mari Sandoz Society Commemorative Issue* (Fall 2005): 1-2.

5. Helen Winter Stauffer, "Mari Sandoz's Status Today," *Prairie Schooner* (Autumn 1990): 35-38.

6. Sandoz to Ed Weeks, 25 October 1949.

7. Stauffer, *The Letters of Mari Sandoz* (Lincoln: University of Nebraska Press, 1992).

8. Charles Nines was an interpreter at Pine Ridge Reservation for several years; he was quite familiar with Lakota language and cultural ways.

9. Mrs. Susan Bordeaux Bettelyoun was of Lakota mixedblood heritage; she kept diaries and memoirs of her childhood as the daughter of a prominent trader. She worked on her autobiography with Josephine Waggoner. *With My Own Eyes: A Lakota Woman Tells Her People's History,* edited by Emily Levine, is the book that eventually grew out of their efforts.

10. Paul Hoffman worked as Sandoz's editor at Knopf; the two remained friends for several years.

11. Henry Alsberg was an editor with Hastings House and had known Sandoz since the 1930s.

12. Bruce Nicoll was the director of the University of Nebraska Press, and helped launch Bison Books. Sandoz fully supported the Bison Book venture and often sent suggestions to Nicoll about which books might be good candidates for the press.

13. Helen Schnidt (or Schmidt, the spelling was difficult to determine) had once been a teacher at a reservation school.

14. Sandoz is referring to the American Indian boarding schools in each of these locations.

15. This is Jules, Jr., Mari's younger brother.

16. Alvin Josephy is an author and historian who has written several books about Native Americans. At this point in time he was a writer for *American Heritage* magazine.

17. Richard B. Williams was a frequent correspondent with Sandoz about Native American historical matters. He worked for the Sturgis public schools, and lobbied to have Bear Butte, near Sturgis, South Dakota, set aside as a state park and historic site.

18. Interestingly, controversy still surrounds White Clay, Nebraska. An unincorporated town of only about fourteen permanent residents, White Clay exists solely to sell alcohol to Lakotas on the neighboring Pine Ridge Reservation. The alcohol sales from this border town generate millions of dollars in revenue each year, causing death and destruction for many Lakota families.

19. The term *berdache* is dated, and carries a negative and derogatory connotation. A more proper term would be *winkte* (specifically for Lakota culture) or "two-spirit" (as a more general term).

CHAPTER 2

1. John Wunder, *"Retained by the People": A History of American Indians and the Bill of Rights* (New York: Oxford University Press, 1994), 99.

2. Vine Deloria, Jr., *Custer Died for Your Sins: An Indian Manifesto* (New York: Macmillan, 1970), 54.

3. Donald L. Parman, *Indians and the American West in the Twentieth Century* (Bloomington: Indiana University Press, 1994), 135.

4. Larry W. Burt, *Tribalism in Crisis: Federal Indian Policy, 1953-1961* (Albuquerque: University of New Mexico Press, 1982), 25.

5. Wunder, *"Retained by the People,"* 110. See also Edward C. Valandra, *Not Without Our Consent: Lakota Resistance to Termination, 1950-59* (Champaign: University of Illinois Press, 2006).

6. Donald L. Fixico, *Termination and Relocation: Federal Indian Policy, 1945-1960* (Albuquerque: University of New Mexico Press, 1986), 94.

7. Kenneth Philp, *Termination Revisited: American Indians on the Trail to Self-Determination, 1933-1953* (Lincoln: University of Nebraska Press, 2002), 89.

8. Burt, *Tribalism in Crisis,* 57.

9. Wilma Mankiller, *Mankiller: A Chief and Her People* (New York: St. Martin's Press, 1993), 71.

10. Angie Debo, *A History of the Indians of the United States* (Norman: University of Oklahoma Press, 1970), 372.

11. Debo, *A History of the Indians*, 374.

12. Burt, *Tribalism in Crisis*, 58.

13. The Van Vleets were close friends of Sandoz, and she often spent time at their Nederland ranch, the Lazy VV, in Colorado.

14. Margaret Marshall was a writer and frequent contributor to *The Nation* magazine.

15. Representative D'Ewart (1889-1973) [Republican, Montana] served several years in both houses of Congress. He favored and promoted termination policies.

16. Dora Wright was an avid Sandoz reader. She wrote to Sandoz of her sister's experiences as a teacher at a reservation school in the 1930s.

17. Mamie Meredith was a good friend of Sandoz's and also longtime English faculty at the University of Nebraska–Lincoln.

18. This was the Merriam Commission report.

19. Myra Peters was an acquaintance of Sandoz's who wrote to her periodically. She was interested in Native American affairs and voiced her concerns to Sandoz in her correspondence.

20. Sandoz is referring to the proposed building of Yellowtail dam on the Big Horn River, a project which would condemn, then flood, a portion of Crow reservation lands in Montana.

21. Finley was a reader of Sandoz's books and a concerned citizen.

22. Leonard Jennewein was field representative for Congressman George McGovern.

23. F. H. Sinclair (aka Neckyoke Jones) was a frequent correspondent with Sandoz. He was instrumental in initiating the "All American Indian Days" Fair and Celebration that was held for many years in Sheridan, WY.

24. Laverne Madigan was the secretary of the Association on American Indian Affairs for several years after the death of Oliver LaFarge. "We Shake Hands" was a program she initiated involving several tribes.

25. Cromwell was a Sandoz reader who was concerned about Native American affairs.

26. Charles Barrett was a frequent correspondent with Sandoz about Native American history. He was also deeply concerned about conditions for Native people, those in the cities and on the reservations.

27. Crazy Horse Monument is an ongoing enterprise. It is the subject of controversy in many Native circles because, while it is supposed to be a tribute to the Oglala Lakota leader, there is significant destruction of sacred land in the Black Hills in order to accomplish the task. The Ziolkowski family is still in charge of the project.

28. Phelps was a reader of Sandoz's books.

29. Sandoz is referring to the Kinzua Dam project in upstate New York, which broke one of the oldest surviving treaties (Sloan-Pickering) with the Six Nations people. It was signed by George Washington and the Seneca leader Cornplanter in 1794.

CHAPTER 3

1. Devon Mihesuah, *Native American Stereotypes and Realities* (Atlanta: Clarity Press, 1996), 9.

2. Jacquelyn Kilpatrick, *Celluloid Indians: Native Americans and Film* (Lincoln: University of Nebraska Press, 1999), 61.

3. Mari Sandoz to Ed Fitzgerald, 31 March 1945, Mari Sandoz Collection, Don L. Love Library, University of Nebraska–Lincoln.

4. Sandoz to Annie Laurie Williams, 12 February 1955.

5. Sandoz memo to Annie Laurie Williams, 28 January 1964.

6. Ralph and Natasha Friar, *The Only Good Indian: The Hollywood Gospel* (New York: Drama Book Specialists, 1972), 2.

7. *Broken Arrow* won the Golden Globe award in 1951 for Promoting International Understanding, and was nominated for three Academy Awards.

8. Louis Owens, *Mixedblood Messages: Literature, Film, Family, Place* (Norman: University of Oklahoma Press, 1998), 100.

9. Sandoz to Father George, 8 June 1962.

10. Sandoz to Wesley D'Ewart, 4 February 1950.

11. Mari Sandoz, *Hostiles and Friendlies* (Lincoln: University of Nebraska Press, 1976), 112.

12. Stauffer, *Mari Sandoz: Story Catcher of the Plains*, 224.

13. Sandoz to Du Mont, 3 October 1953.

14. Sandoz had been asked to appear on a television interview for WJZ-TV in New York to dispel stereotypes most Americans held about American Indian people.

15. Helen Hayes, a good friend of Sandoz's, was a columnist for the *Lincoln Star*.

16. Annie Laurie Williams handled the movie rights to Sandoz's books.

17. Rosebud Yellow Robe was a young Lakota actress, writer, and activist from South Dakota. Her father was Chauncey Yellow Robe, a well known Lakota orator and statesman.

18. Yust is most likely referring to the "Sioux Uprising" of 1862 which occurred at New Ulm, Minnesota. Sandoz is correct in saying Sitting Bull (Hunkpapa) had nothing to do with the happenings there, as he was located far to the west in the Upper Missouri country.

19. Mary Abbot worked for Sandoz's literary firm, MacIntosh and Otis. She handled most of the novelists represented by the firm and worked closely with Sandoz.

20. Although this is a memo rather than a letter, I felt it important to include here as it points out several issues Sandoz had with Hollywood's portrayal of Native people in the film industry.

CHAPTER 4

1. Quoted in Richard White, *It's Your Misfortune and None of My Own: A New History of the American West* (Norman: University of Oklahoma Press, 1993), 622.

2. Mari Sandoz to Major Edward S. Luce, 15 September 1952.

3. Joseph Traugott, "Native American Artists and the Postmodern Cultural Divide," *Art Journal* (Fall 1992): 36.

4. Margaret Archuleta, Heard Museum, and Rennard Strickland, *Shared Visions: Native American Painters and Sculptors in the Twentieth Century* (Phoenix: New Press, 1991), 30.

5. Ruth Phillips, "Art History and the Native-made Object," in W. Jackson Rushing III, *Native American Art in the Twentieth Century: Makers, Meanings, Histories* (London: Routledge, 1999), 103.

6. Stauffer, *Mari Sandoz: Story Catcher of the Plains*, 178.

7. Sandoz to Sandcrane, 9 May 1950.

8. Sandoz to Sandcrane, 9 May 1950.

9. Margot Liberty to author, telephone interview, 22 May 2003.

10. Sandoz to Brummett Echohawk, 10 April 1954.

11. Stauffer, *Mari Sandoz: Story Catcher of the Plains*, 179.

12. University of Wisconsin News Service, 21 August 1950.

13. Father Powell, letter to author, 3 June 2003.

14. Raymond DeMallie to Sandoz, 25 January 1962.

15. University of Indiana website, "Chancellor's Professor of Anthropology and American Indian Studies." Accessed 24 May 2008.

16. Sandoz is referring to *The Life and Adventures of Frank Grouard* by Joe De-Barthe, first published in 1894.

17. Elizabeth Otis, of the firm MacIntosh and Otis, was Sandoz's literary agent for many years.

18. Sandoz taught summer sessions at University of Wisconsin for aspiring novelists and students.

19. Margot Liberty is an anthropologist, historian, and writer closely associated with the Northern Cheyennes. She coauthored *Cheyenne Memories* with John Stands in Timber.

20. Hila Gilbert was a close acquaintance of Sandoz's who worked closely with the Northern Cheyenne tribe in Montana.

21. This was a small monetary award that Sandoz set up during her lifetime to help encourage young Native artists among the Northern Cheyennes.

22. Walter Frese, a partner with Henry Alsberg at Hastings House, was always interested in finding new writers to contribute to their Western Americana lists. Sandoz usually sent notes like these to them to let them know of "new talent."

AFTERWORD

1. Vine Deloria, Jr., Introduction to *Crazy Horse: Strange Man of the Oglalas* (Lincoln: University of Nebraska Press, 2004), v-xv.

2. Ibid.

BIBLIOGRAPHY

Archuleta, Margaret, and Rennard Strickland. *Shared Visions: Native American Painters in the Twentieth Century.* Phoenix: Heard Museum, 1991.

Arnold, Elliot. *Blood Brother.* New York: Duell, Sloan and Pearce, 1947.

Bataille, Gretchen, and Charles Silet. *The Pretend Indians: Images of Native Americans in the Movies.* Ames: University of Iowa Press, 1980.

Blish, Helen. *A Pictographic History of the Oglala Sioux: Drawings by Amos Bad Heart Bull.* Lincoln: University of Nebraska Press, 1967.

Broken Arrow. Delmer Daves, director, 20th Century Fox; 1950.

Brown, Joseph Epes, ed. and recorder, and Nicholas Black Elk. *The Sacred Pipe: The Seven Sacred Rites of the Oglala Sioux.* Norman: University of Oklahoma Press, 1953.

Burt, Larry W. *Tribalism in Crisis: Federal Indian Policy, 1953–1961.* Albuquerque: University of New Mexico Press, 1982.

Cheyenne Autumn. John Ford, director, Warner Brothers; 1964.

Chief Crazy Horse. George Sherman, director, Universal Pictures; 1955.

Churchill, Ward. *Fantasies of the Master Race.* San Francisco: City Lights, 1998.

The Comancheros. Michael Curtis and John Wayne, directors, 20th Century Fox; 1961.

Debo, Angie. *A History of the Indians of the United States.* Norman: University of Oklahoma Press, 1970.

Deloria, Vine, Jr. *Custer Died for Your Sins: An Indian Manifesto.* New York: Macmillan, 1970.

———. "Introduction." *Crazy Horse: Strange Man of the Oglalas.* Lincoln: University of Nebraska Press, 2004.

Downey, Betsy. "She Does Not Write Like a Historian: Mari Sandoz and the Old and New Western History." *Great Plains Quarterly* (Winter 1996): 9–25.

Fixico, Donald L. *Termination and Relocation: Federal Indian Policy, 1945–1960.* Albuquerque: University of New Mexico Press, 1986.

Forbes, Jack D. *Apache, Navaho, and Spaniard.* Norman: University of Oklahoma Press, 1960.

Fort Apache. John Ford, director, Warner Brothers; 1948.

Friar, Ralph and Natasha. *The Only Good Indian: The Hollywood Gospel.* New York: Drama Book Specialists, 1972.

Kenny, Maurice. *Dead Letters Sent and Other Poems.* New York: Troubador Press, 1958.

Kilpatrick, Jacquelyn. *Celluloid Indians: Native Americans and Film.* Lincoln: University of Nebraska Press, 1999.

Mankiller, Wilma. *Mankiller: A Chief and Her People.* New York: St. Martin's Press, 1993.

Mathews, John Joseph. *Osages: Children of the Middle Waters.* Norman: University of Oklahoma Press, 1961.

———. *The Life and Death of an Oilman: The Career of E. W. Marland.* Norman: University of Oklahoma Press, 1951.

McNickle, D'Arcy. *They Came Here First.* Philadelphia: Lippincott, 1949.

Mihesuah, Devon. *Native American Stereotypes and Realities.* Atlanta: Clarity, 1996.

Momaday, N. Scott. *House Made of Dawn.* New York: Harper and Row, 1968.

Owens, Louis. *Mixedblood Messages: Literature, Film, Family, Place.* Norman: University of Oklahoma Press, 1998.

Parman, Donald L. *Indians and the American West in the Twentieth Century.* Bloomington: Indiana University Press, 1994.

Phillips, Ruth. "Art History and the Native-made Object," in W. Jackson Rushing III, *Native American Art in the Twentieth Century: Makers, Meanings, Histories.* London: Routledge, 1999, 103.

Philp, Kenneth. *Termination Revisited: American Indians on the Trail to Self-Determination, 1933–1953.* Lincoln: University of Nebraska Press, 2002.

Polingays, Qoyawama. *No Turning Back.* Albuquerque: New Mexico University Press, 1964.

Powell, Peter J. *People of the Sacred Mountain.* New York: Harper and Row, 1981.

———. *Sweet Medicine.* Norman: University of Oklahoma Press, 1969.

Prucha, Francis Paul. *Documents of United States Indian Policy.* Lincoln: University of Nebraska Press, 2000.

Sandoz, Mari. *Cheyenne Autumn.* (1953) Lincoln: University of Nebraska Press, 1992.

———. *Crazy Horse: Strange Man of the Oglalas* (1942). New York: Hastings House, 1970.

———. *Hostiles and Friendlies*. Lincoln: University of Nebraska Press, 1976.

———. *Old Jules*. New York: Little Brown, 1932.

———. "There Were Two Sitting Bulls." *Blue Book*, 90 (November 1949): 58–65.

———. *These Were the Sioux*. New York: Hastings House, 1961.

The Searchers. John Ford, director, Warner Brothers; 1956.

Sitting Bull. Sidney Salkow, director, W. R. Frank Productions; 1954.

Stauffer, Helen Winter. *Mari Sandoz: Story Catcher of the Plains*. Lincoln: University of Nebraska Press, 1982.

Traugott, Joseph. "Native American Artists and the Postmodern Cultural Divide." *Art Journal* (Fall 1992): 36.

Voorhees, Richard. "Professor Fling 'Difficult' but Essential to Mari's Historical Methods." *One Drop: Mari Sandoz Society Commemorative Issue* (Spring 2003): 8–9.

———. "John D. Hicks and Mari Sandoz." *One Drop: Mari Sandoz Society Commemorative Issue* (Fall 2005): 1–2.

White, Richard. *It's Your Misfortune and None of My Own*. Norman: University of Oklahoma Press, 1991.

Wunder, John *"Retained by the People": A History of American Indians and the Bill of Rights*. New York: Oxford University Press, 1994.

ARCHIVAL MATERIALS

Mari Sandoz Correspondence (1940–1965). Special Collections, Love Library; University of Nebraska–Lincoln.

INTERVIEWS

Margot Liberty. Telephone Interview. May 22, 2003.

Caroline Sandoz Pifer. Personal Interview. April 10, 2003.

Powell, Peter J. Telephone Interview. May 5, 2006.

CORRESPONDENCE

Powell, Peter J. Letter to author. June 3, 2003.

———. Letter to author. June 13, 2003.

———

Page numbers in *italics* indicate
photographs.

* * *